The Seagull Sartre Library

The Seagull Sartre Library

VOLUME 1

Post-War Reflections

VOLUME 2

On Revolution

VOLUME 3

On Poetry

VOLUME 4

Political Fictions

VOLUME 5

On Merleau-Ponty

VOLUME 6

Venice and Rome

VOLUME 7

On Modern Art

VOLUME 8

On Camus

VOLUME 9

Occasional Philosophical Writings

VOLUME 10

On Bataille and Blanchot

VOLUME 11

On Novels and Novelists

VOLUME 12

On American Fiction

The Seagull Sartre Library

VOLUME 2
ON REVOLUTION

JEAN-PAUL SARTRE

TRANSLATED BY
CHRIS TURNER

LONDON NEW YORK CALCUTTA

This work is published with the support of
Institut français en Inde – Embassy of France in India

Seagull Books, 2021

Originally published in Jean-Paul Sartre,
Situations III © Éditions Gallimard, Paris, new edition, 2003, and
Situations IV © Éditions Gallimard, Paris, 1964

These essays were first published in English translation
by Seagull Books in *The Aftermath of War* (2008) and *Portraits* (2009)

English translation © Chris Turner, 2008, 2009

ISBN 978 0 8574 2 905 6

British Library Cataloguing-in-Publication Data
A catalogue record for this book is available
from the British Library

Typeset by Seagull Books, Calcutta, India
Printed and bound in the USA

CONTENTS

1
Materialism and Revolution

92
The Artist and His Conscience

118
A Note on the Sources

✳

MATERIALISM AND REVOLUTION[1]

I. THE REVOLUTIONARY MYTH

Today's youth are uneasy. They no longer feel entitled to be young and it is as though youth were not an age of life but a class phenomenon, an unduly prolonged childhood, an additional period of irresponsibility granted to the children of the middle classes. The workers pass without transition from adolescence to manhood. And it seems that our times, which are eliminating the European bourgeoisies, are also eliminating that abstract, metaphysical period which was always said to be due 'its fling'. Out of shame at their youth and that footloose quality that was once the fashion, most of my ex-students have married young: they have families while they are still studying. At the

---

1 As I have been unfairly charged with not quoting Marx in this article, I should like to point out that my criticisms are not directed against him, but against the Marxist scholasticism of 1949. Or, if one prefers, against Marx through Stalinist neo-Marxism.

end of each month they still receive a postal order from their families, but it is not enough. They have to give lessons or translate or do supply teaching. They are half-workers, comparable in part to kept women and in part to homeworkers. They no longer take the time, as we did at their age, to play with ideas before adopting one. They are fathers and citizens; they vote; they have to commit themselves. This is doubtless no bad thing. After all, it is right they should be asked to choose from the outset whether they are for or against humanity, for or against the masses. But, if they take the former option, the difficulties begin, because they become persuaded that they have to slough off their subjectivity. If they contemplate doing this, however, being still inside their subjectivity, they do so for reasons that remain subjective. They consult themselves before plunging themselves into the water and, as a result, the more seriously they contemplate abandoning their subjectivity, the greater the importance it assumes. And they come to see, with some irritation, that their conception of objectivity is still a subjective one. And so they go round and round, unable to make a decision and, if they do make up their minds, they jump blindly for reasons of weariness or impatience.

Yet that is not an end to it. They are now being told to choose between materialism and idealism. They are told there is no middle way; it must be the one or the other. Yet, for most of them the principles of materialism seem philosophically false. They cannot understand how matter could give rise to the idea of matter. They protest, however, that they reject idealism with all their might and main; they know it is a myth that serves the propertied classes and that it is not a rigorous philosophy but quite a vague form of thinking, the function of which is to mask reality or absorb it into the idea. 'It makes no difference,' they are told. 'Since you are not materialists, you will be idealists in spite of yourselves and, though you resist the stale ruses of the academics, you will fall victim to a more subtle and even more dangerous illusion.'

So they are hounded even in their thoughts, which are poisoned at the roots, being condemned either to serve a philosophy they detest or, for reasons of discipline, adopt a doctrine in which they cannot believe. They have lost the carefree attitude proper to their age without acquiring the certainty of maturity. They are no longer footloose and yet they cannot commit themselves. They remain at the gates of Communism without daring to either enter or leave. They are not guilty: it is not their fault if the very people who invoke the dialectic want to force them to choose between two opposites and reject with the scornful name of Third Party the synthesis that would embrace the two. Since they are deeply sincere, since they wish to see a socialist regime, since they are ready to serve the Revolution with all their might, the only way to help them is to ask oneself, with them, whether materialism and the myth of objectivity are really demanded by the cause of the Revolution and whether there isn't a discrepancy between the revolutionary's actions and his ideology. For this reason, I turn now to materialism and attempt to examine it once again.

It seems that materialism's first move is to deny the existence of God and transcendent finality, its second to reduce the action of mind to that of matter, its third to eliminate subjectivity by reducing the world, with man in it, to a system of objects interconnected by universal relations. I conclude from this, in all good faith, that it is a metaphysical doctrine and that the materialists are metaphysicians. This is where they stop me right away: I am wrong, they say; there is nothing they hate so much as metaphysics. It is not even clear that philosophy is spared in their eyes. According to M. Naville, dialectical materialism is 'the expression of a progressive discovery of the world's interactions, a discovery that is in no way passive but involves the activity of the discoverer, the seeker and the struggler'. According to M. Garaudy, materialism's first move is to deny that there is any legitimate knowledge apart from scientific knowledge. And, for Mme Angrand, one cannot be a materialist unless one first rejects all a priori speculation.

These reproaches against metaphysics are old acquaintances: we met them in the last century in the writings of the positivists. But they, being more consistent, refused to pronounce on the existence of God because they regarded any conjectures one might form on that subject as unverifiable. And they had given up once and for all enquiring into the relations between mind and body, because they thought we could know nothing about it. It is clear, in fact, that M. Naville or Mme Angrand's atheism is not 'the expression of a progressive discovery'. It is a clear, a priori stance on a problem that infinitely exceeds our experience. Their position is also my own, but I did not see myself as any less of a metaphysician in denying existence to God than Leibniz was in granting it. And by what miracle would the materialist who criticizes the idealists for engaging in metaphysics when they reduce matter to spirit not be doing precisely the same thing when he reduces spirit to matter? Experience does not rule in favour of his doctrine any more than it does in favour of the opposing one. It confines itself to displaying the intimate connection between the physiological and the psychical, and that connection may be interpreted in a thousand different ways. When the materialist claims to be certain of his principles, his assurance can come only from a priori reasoning or intuition—in other words, from those very speculations he condemns. I understand now that materialism is a metaphysics hiding behind a positivism; but it is a self-destructive metaphysics, since, by undermining metaphysics on principle, it deprives its own assertions of any foundation.

By the same token, it destroys the positivism behind which it takes cover. It was out of modesty that Comte's disciples reduced human knowledge to scientific learning alone: they confined reason within the narrow limits of our experience because it was only there that it showed itself to be effective. For them, the success of science was a fact, but it was a human fact. From the human standpoint, and for human beings, it is true that science succeeds. They were careful not to ask themselves whether the universe in itself supports and underwrites scientific rationalism, for the very good reason that they would have been obliged to step outside themselves and humanity to compare the universe as it is with the representation science provides of it and to assume the vantage point of God on man and the world. The materialist, for his part, is not so timid. He steps outside science, subjectivity and the human, and substitutes himself for the God he denies in order to contemplate the spectacle of the universe. He calmly writes, 'The materialistic outlook on nature means no more than simply conceiving nature just as it exists, without any foreign admixture.'[2]

---

2 Karl Marx and Friedrich Engels, *Complete Works* (New York: International Publishers, 1980), VOL. 14, p. 651. I quote this text for the use that is being made of it today. I propose to

What is happening, in this surprising text, is nothing short of the suppression of human subjectivity, that 'foreign admixture'. The materialist thinks that, by denying his subjectivity, he has made it vanish. But the trick performed here is an easy one to spot. In order to eliminate subjectivity, the materialist declares himself to be an object, that is to say, material for science. But once he has eliminated subjectivity in favour of the object, instead of seeing himself as a thing among other things, buffeted about by the undertow of the physical universe, he turns himself into an objective observer and claims to contemplate nature as it is, in the absolute. There is a play on the word 'objectivity' here; at times it means the passive quality of the object under observation and at others, the absolute value of an observer shorn of subjective weaknesses. So the materialist, having transcended all subjectivity and identified himself with pure objective truth, moves around in a world of objects inhabited by human objects. And when he returns from his travels, he reports what he has learnt: 'All that is rational is real,' he tells us, 'and all that is real is rational.'

Where does he get this rationalistic optimism? We can understand a Kantian making declarations about nature, since, in his view, reason constitutes experience. But the materialist does not accept that the

demonstrate elsewhere that Marx had a much deeper and richer conception of objectivity.

world is the product of our constitutive activity. On the contrary, in his eyes it is we who are the product of the universe. Why, then, would we know that the real is rational, since we have not created it and reflect only a tiny part of it from day to day. At a pinch the success of science may lead us to think that this rationality is probable, but it may be a question of a local, statistical rationality. It may be valid for a certain order of magnitude and collapse above or below that limit.

Out of something which seems to us a reckless induction or, if you prefer, a postulate, materialism makes a certainty. For materialism there is no doubt. Reason is within man and outside him. And the leading journal of materialism calmly calls itself La Pensée [Thought], 'the organ of modern rationalism'. However, by a quite foreseeable dialectical reversal, materialist rationalism goes over into irrationalism and destroys itself: if the psychological fact is rigorously conditioned by the biological, and the biological fact is conditioned in turn by the physical state of the world, I can quite see how human consciousness may express the universe in the way an effect expresses its cause but not in the way a thought expresses its object. How could a reason that was captive, externally governed and manipulated by sequences of blind causes, still be reason? How could I believe in the principles of my deductions if it were merely external events that had deposited them in me and if, as Hegel says, 'reason is a bone'?[3] By what stroke of chance would the raw products of circumstance at the same time provide the keys to Nature? Moreover, look how Lenin speaks of our consciousness: 'It is merely the reflection of being—in the best of cases, an approximately exact reflection.' But who is to decide whether the present case—here, materialism—is the best of cases? We would have to be both outside and inside to make the comparison. And, as there can be no question of this, by the very terms of our declaration we have no criterion for the validity of the reflection, except internal, subjective criteria: its conformity with other reflections, its clarity, distinctness and permanence. In short, idealist criteria. And, even then, these will only determine a truth for human beings; and that truth, not being constructed like the truth proposed by the Kantians but received passively, will never be anything but a faith without foundation and a matter of habit.

Though dogmatic when it asserts that the universe produces thought, materialism goes over immediately into idealist scepticism. It lays down the inalienable rights of Reason with the one hand and takes them away with the other. It destroys positivism with a dogmatic rationalism, destroys both of these by the metaphysical assertion that man is a material

3 Hegel's exact words seem to have been: 'Der Geist ist ein Knochen'—spirit is a bone. [Trans.]

object and destroys this assertion with the radical negation of all metaphysics. It pits science against metaphysics and, without realizing it, pits a meta-physics against science. Only ruins are left. How then could I be a materialist?

It will be objected that I have understood nothing, that I have confused the naive materialism of Helvétius and d'Holbach with dialectical materialism. There is, I am told, a dialectical movement within nature whereby opposites, as they clash, are suddenly overcome and united in a new synthesis. And this new production goes over in turn into its opposite, to merge with it in another synthesis. I recognize at once the characteristic movement of the Hegelian dialectic here, a dialectic based entirely on the dynamism of Ideas. I recall how, in Hegel's philosophy, one idea leads to another, how each one produces its opposite. I know that the driving force behind this immense movement is the attraction exerted by the future on the present and by the whole, even when it does not exist yet, on its parts. This is as true of partial syntheses as it is of the absolute Totality, which ultimately will be Mind or Spirit [Geist]. The principle of this Dialec-tic is, then, that a whole governs its parts; that an idea tends of itself to complete and enrich itself; that the progress of consciousness is not linear, like that of cause and effect, but synthetic and multi-dimensional, since each idea retains within itself and assimilates to itself the totality of previous ideas; that the structure of the concept is not the mere juxtaposition of invariable elements which could, if need be, join with other elements to produce new combinations, but an organization whose unity is such that its secondary structures could not be considered in isolation from the whole without becoming 'abstract' and losing their nature.

One readily accepts this dialectic in the realm of ideas: ideas are naturally synthetic. Only, we are told, Hegel had stood it on its head and it is, in reality, specific to matter. And if you ask what matter we are speaking of, you are told that there is only one—the matter of which scientists speak. Now, matter is characterized by its inertia. That means it is incapable of producing anything by itself. It is a vehicle for movement and energy, but that movement and energy always come to it from outside: it borrows them and yields them up again. The mainspring of all dialectics is the idea of totality. In dialectics, phenomena are never isolated occurrences; when they occur together, they do so always within the higher unity of a whole and they are connected by internal relations, that is to say, the presence of one modifies the other in its deep nature. But the world of science is quantitative. And quantity is precisely the opposite of dialectical unity. Only in appearance is a sum a unity. The elements that make it up have, in fact, only relations of continuity and simultaneity between them. They are present together, and that is all. A numerical unit is in no sense influenced by the co-presence of another unit; it remains inert and separate within the number it helps to form. And things have to be this way if we are to be able to count. For if two phenomena occurred in intimate union and modified each other reciprocally, it would be impossible to decide whether we were dealing with two separate terms or with one. Thus, as scientific matter represents, so to speak, the realization of quantity, science is, in its inmost concerns, its principles and its methods, the opposite of dialectics.

When science speaks of forces that are applied at a material point, its first concern is to assert their independence: each acts as though it were alone. If it studies the attraction bodies exert on one another, it is careful to define that attraction as a strictly external relation or, in other words, to reduce it to changes in the direction and velocity of their movements. Science occasionally uses the word 'synthesis', for example in relation to chemical combinations. But it never does so in the Hegelian sense. The particles that come into combination retain their properties; if an atom of oxygen combines with atoms of sulphur and hydrogen to form sulphuric acid or with hydrogen alone to form water, it remains identical to itself. Neither the water nor the acid are genuine totalities that change and govern their components. They are mere passive resultants or states. The entire effort of biology is aimed at reducing alleged living syntheses to physico-chemical processes. And when M. Naville, who is a materialist, feels the need to create a materialist psychology, he turns to 'behaviourism', which regards human conduct as a sum of conditioned reflexes. Nowhere in the world of science do we meet any organic totalities. The scientist's tool is analysis; his aim is everywhere to reduce the complex to the simple and the recomposition he subsequently effects is simply a countercheck, whereas the dialectician, on principle, regards complexes as irreducible.

Admittedly, Engels claims that, 'nature is the test of dialectics, and it must be said for modern natural science that it has furnished . . . materials for this test, and has thus proved that in the last analysis nature's process is dialectical and not metaphysical, that it does not move in an eternal uniform and constantly repeated circle, but passes through a real history.'[4] And he cites the example of Darwin to support his argument: '(Darwin) dealt a severe blow to the metaphysical conception of nature by proving that the organic world of today . . . is all a product of a process of development that has been in progress for millions of

4 Friedrich Engels, *Socialism, Utopian and Scientific*, Chapter 2, 'Dialectics' (New York: International Publishers, 1972), p. 48.

years.'[5] But first it is clear that the notion of natural history is absurd. History is characterized neither by change nor by the pure and simple action of the past; it is defined by the intentional re-appropriation of the past by the present: there can only be a human history. Besides, if Darwin has shown that species derive from one another, his attempt to explain this is of a mechanical, not a dialectical, order. He accounts for individual differences by the theory of small variations. And each of these variations is, in his view, not in fact the effect of a 'process of development' but of mechanical chance. Statistically, it is impossible in a group of individuals of a same species for there not to be some that are greater in size, weight, strength or some particular detail. As for the struggle for existence, it cannot produce a new synthesis by merging opposites; it has strictly negative effects, since it eliminates the weakest once and for all. To grasp this, we need only compare the outcome with the truly dialectical ideal of the class struggle. In the latter case, the proletariat will merge the bourgeois class into itself in the unity of a classless society. In the struggle for existence, the strong purely and simply wipe out the weak. Lastly, the chance advantage does not develop: it remains inert and is passed on unchanged by heredity. It is a state and that state will not modify itself by an

---

5 Engels, *Socialism*, p. 48.

inner dynamism to produce a higher degree of organization. Another chance variation will simply be added
to it from outside and the process of elimination will
be reproduced mechanically. Should we conclude
from this that Engels is being frivolous or dishonest?
In order to prove that nature has a history, he employs
a scientific hypothesis explicitly intended to reduce all
natural history to mechanical sequences.

Is Engels more serious when he speaks of physics?

'In physics . . . every change is a passing of quantity into quality, as a result of quantitative change of
some form of movement either inherent in a body or
imparted to it. "For example, the temperature of water
has at first no effect on its liquid state; but as the temperature of liquid water rises or falls, a moment arrives
when this state of cohesion changes and the water
is converted in one case into steam and in the other
into ice." '6

But he is confusing us here with smoke and mir-
rors. Scientific research is not at all concerned, in fact,
with demonstrating the transition from quantity to
quality. It starts out from the perceptible quality, conceived as an illusory, subjective appearance, in order

6 Sartre does not reference this passage, which is from *The
Dialectics of Nature* (1940). Following Engels, he also fails to
note that the words from 'For example . . .' onwards are from
Section 108 of Hegel's *Logic* (Oxford: Clarendon, 1978, pp.
158–9), though the translation differs slightly. [Trans.]

to discover the quantity behind it that is conceived as the truth of the universe. Engels naively regards quantity as though it presented itself initially as a pure quantity. But, in fact, it first appears as a quality: it is that state of unease or contentment that makes us button up our raincoat or, conversely, take it off. The scientist reduced this perceptible quality to a quantity when he agreed to substitute for the vague message from our senses the measurement of the cubic expansion of a liquid. The transformation of water into steam is an equally quantitative phenomenon for him. Or, to put it another way, it exists for him only as quantity. It is by pressure that he will define steam— or by a kinetic theory that will reduce it to a certain quantitative state (position or velocity) of its molecules. We must, then, choose. Either we remain on the ground of the perceptible quality and steam is then a quality, as also is temperature; we are not doing science, but are observing the action of one quality on another. Or we view temperature as a quantity, but then the transition from the liquid to the gaseous state will be defined scientifically as a quantitative change—that is to say, by a measurable pressure exerted on a piston or by measurable relations between molecules. For the scientist, quantity produces quantity; the law is a quantitative formula and science has no symbol at its disposal to express quality as such. What Engels claims to present to us as a scientific approach is the pure and simple movement of his mind which goes from the scientific universe to that of naive realism and then returns to the scientific world to recover the world of pure sensation. And even if we conceded all this to him, does this toing-and-froing of thought in the least resemble a dialectical process? Where does he see a progression? Let us accept that the change of temperature, regarded as quantitative, produces a qualitative transformation of water: water is changed into steam. What then? It will exert pressure on an escape valve and open it; it will rise into the air, cool and become water again. Where is the progression? I see a cycle. Of course, water is no longer contained in the recipient but is outside on the grass and earth in the form of dew. But by what metaphysics can one see this change of place as an advance?[7]

It will perhaps be objected that some modern theories, such as Einstein's, are synthetic. In his system,

---

7 There is no way out of this problem by speaking of intensive quantities. Bergson long ago exposed the confusions and errors in this myth that was the undoing of the psycho-physicists. Temperature, insofar as it is felt by us, is a quality. It is not hotter than it was yesterday, but differently hot. And, conversely, the degree, measured in terms of cubic expansion, is a pure and simply quantity to which there remains attached, in the mind of the layman, a vague idea of a perceptible quality. Modern physics, far from retaining this ambiguous notion, reduces heat to certain atomic motions. Where, then, is the intensity? And what is the intensity of a sound or of light but a mathematical relation?

as we know, there are no longer any isolated elements: every reality is defined in relation to the universe. There is much that could be said about this but I shall confine myself to observing that what we have here is not a synthesis at all, since the relations that can be established between the various structures of a synthesis are internal and qualitative whereas the relations that enable us to define a position or a mass in Einstein's theories remain quantitative and external. Moreover, this is not the key point. Whether we are speaking of Newton, Archimedes, Laplace or Einstein, the scientist does not study the concrete totality but the general and abstract conditions of the universe. Not this event, which takes light, heat and life and melds them into something particular, known as 'the glistening of the sun through foliage on a summer's day', but light in general, calorific phenomena, the general conditions of life. It is not a question of examining this refraction through this piece of glass which has its history and which, from a certain standpoint, can be seen as the concrete synthesis of the universe, but the conditions of possibility of refraction in general. Science is made up of concepts in the Hegelian sense of the term. Dialectics, on the other hand, is essentially the play of notions. We know that, in Hegel's conception, the notion organizes and fuses together concepts in the organic, living unity of concrete reality. The Earth, the Renaissance, Colonization in the nineteenth century and Nazism are understood as notions; Being, Light and Energy are abstract concepts. Dialectical enrichment lies in the passage from abstract to concrete, that is to say, from elementary concepts to ever more complex notions. Thus, the movement of the dialectic is the reverse of the movement of science.

'It's true,' a Communist intellectual admitted to me, 'that science and dialectics pull in opposite directions. But this is because science expresses the bourgeois viewpoint, which is analytical. Our dialectic, by contrast, is the very thinking of the proletariat.' I can accept this, though Soviet science doesn't seem to differ very much in its methods from the science of the bourgeois states. But if this is the case, why do the Communists borrow arguments and evidence from science on which to base their materialism? The basic spirit of science is, I believe, materialistic. But here we are told that it is analytic and bourgeois. The positions are, as a result, reversed and I can clearly see two classes in struggle: the one, the bourgeoisie, is materialist, its method of thinking is analytic, its ideology is science; the other, the proletariat, is idealist, its method of thinking is synthesis, its ideology is dialectics. And since there is struggle between the classes, there must be incompatibility between the ideologies. But not at all: we are told that dialectics is the crowning glory of science and makes use of its results; we are told that the bourgeoisie, drawing on analysis and, consequently, reducing the higher to the lower, is idealist, whereas the proletariat—which thinks in terms of synthesis and is led by the revolutionary ideal— even though it asserts the irreducibility of a synthesis to its elements, is materialist. Who can make any sense of all this?

Let us come back, then, to science which, whether it is bourgeois or not, has at least proved itself. We know what it teaches about matter. A material object, which is animated from without, conditioned by the total state of the world, subject to forces that always have their origin elsewhere, and made up of elements that combine without interpenetrating and remain alien to it, is external to itself; its most evident properties are statistical; they are merely the resultant of the motion of the molecules that make it up. Nature, as Hegel so profoundly says, is externality. How are we to find a place in this externality for that movement of absolute internalization that is dialectics? Is it not clear from the very idea of synthesis that life is irreducible to matter and human consciousness irreducible to life? Between modern science, object of materialist faith and love, and the dialectics the materialists claim as their instrument and method, there is the same discrepancy as we noted above between their positivism and their metaphysics: the one wrecks the other. And so they will tell you at one point that life is merely a complex sequence of physico-chemical phenomena and at another, with the same imperturbability, that it is an irreducible moment of the natural dialectic. Or, rather, they attempt, dishonestly to think both at the same time. One has the sense, from their confused discourse, that they have invented the slippery, contradictory notion of reducible irreducibilities.

M. Garaudy is satisfied with this. But when you hear him speak you are struck by his wavering: at times he asserts, in the abstract, that mechanistic determinism has had its day and that it must be replaced by dialectics; at others, when he attempts to explain a concrete situation, he comes back to causal relations, which are linear and presuppose the absolute externality of the cause to the effect. It is perhaps this notion of cause that best shows up the great intellectual confusion into which the materialists have fallen. When I challenged M. Naville to define, within the framework of the dialectic, this famous causality he is so fond of employing, he seemed disconcerted and had no reply. How well I understand him! I would be inclined to say that the notion of cause remains hanging between scientific relations and dialectical syntheses. Materialism being, as we have seen, an explanatory metaphysics (it attempts to explain some social phenomena by others, the psychological sphere by the biological, the biological by physico-chemical laws), it uses the causal schema on principle. But, since it sees science as the explanation of the universe, it turns to science and is surprised to find that the causal connection is not scientific. Where is the cause in Joule's Law or Mariotte's, in Archimedes' Principle or Carnot's? Science most often establishes functional relations between phenomena and chooses the independent variable that suits its purpose. It is, moreover, strictly impossible to express the qualitative relation of causality in mathematical language. Most physical laws simply take the form of functions of the type $y = f(x)$. Others establish numerical constants. Yet others give us phases of irreversible phenomena, but without our being able to say that one of these phases is the cause of the next (can we say that in karyokinesis, nuclear dissolution is the cause of the segmentation of the protoplasmic filament?). So materialist causality remains up in the air. The fact is that it has its origin in the metaphysical attempt to reduce mind to matter and explain the psychological by the physical. Disappointed that there is too little in science to bolster his causal explanations, the materialist reverts, then, to the dialectic. But there is too much in the dialectic. The causal link is linear and the cause remains external to its effect. Moreover, there is never more in the effect than in the cause: otherwise, from the standpoint of causal explanation, that residue would remain unexplained. Dialectical progress, by contrast, is a totalizing progress: at each new stage it looks back on the set of positions transcended and embraces them all. And the move from one stage to another is always an enrichment: there is always more in the synthesis than in the thesis and antithesis combined. So the materialists' cause can neither be backed by science nor hang itself on the dialectic: it remains a vulgar, practical notion, the mark of materialism's unceasing effort to bend the one towards the other and unite two mutually exclusive methods by force; it is the very type of the false synthesis and the use made of it is a dishonest one.

Nowhere is this more evident than in the Marxists' attempts to study 'superstructures'. For Marxists, these are, in a sense, 'reflections' of the mode of production.

Hence, if in different periods of the history of society different social ideas, theories, views and political institutions are to be observed; if under the slave system we encounter certain social ideas, theories, views and political institutions, under feudalism others, and under capitalism others still, this is not to be explained by the 'nature', the 'properties' of the ideas, theories, views and political institutions themselves but by the different conditions of the material life of society at different periods of social development. Whatever is the being of a society, whatever are the conditions of material life of a society, such are the ideas, theories, political views and political institutions of that society.[8]

The use of the term 'reflection' and that of the verb 'determine', together with the general tone of the passage, tell us all we need to know: we are on the terrain of determinism; the superstructure is entirely supported and conditioned by the social situation it reflects; the relation of the mode of production to the political institution is one of cause to effect. It was on this basis that a naive thinker once saw Spinoza's philosophy as an exact reflection of the Dutch grain trade. But at the same time, because Marxist propaganda needs it to be this way, ideologies must, to a degree, have a certain self-sufficiency and be able to act back on the social situation that conditions them. This means, in short, that they must have a certain autonomy from the substructures. For this reason, Marxists have recourse here to the dialectic and present the superstructure as a synthesis which, though it emanates from the conditions of production and material life, has a nature and laws of development that are genuinely 'independent'. In the same pamphlet, Stalin writes:

> New social ideas and theories arise only after the development of the material life of society has set new tasks before society . . . New social

8 Vladimir Ilich Stalin, *Dialectical and Historical Materialism* (New York: International Publishers, 1940[1938]), p. 21.

ideas and theories arise precisely because they are necessary to society, because it is impossible to carry out the urgent tasks of development of the material life of society without their organizing, mobilizing and transforming action.[9]

In this text, necessity has, as we see, assumed a quite different aspect: an idea arises because it is necessary for the accomplishment of a new task. In other words, the task, before even being accomplished, calls forth the idea that will 'facilitate' its accomplishment. The idea is postulated and arises out of a vacuum which it then fills. The word 'arise' is actually the one Stalin uses a few lines later. This action of the future, this necessity which is coterminous with purpose, this organizing, mobilizing and transforming power of the idea clearly brings us back to the terrain of the Hegelian dialectic. But how can I believe in both of Stalin's assertions at once? Is the idea 'determined by the social situation' or 'arising out of the new tasks to be accomplished'? Should we believe with him that 'the spiritual life of society is a reflection of [this] objective reality, a reflection of being'—that is to say, a derived, borrowed reality, that has no being of its own but is more or less analogous to the Stoics' 'lecta'?

---

9 Stalin, *Dialectical and Historical Materialism*, pp. 22–3. My emphasis.

Or should I, rather, declare with Lenin that 'ideas become living realities when they live in the consciousness of the masses'? On the one hand, a causal and linear relation, implying the inertia of the effect or reflection and on the other a dialectical, synthetic relation which would imply that the final synthesis turns back to the partial syntheses that have produced it to embrace them and merge them into itself; therefore, that mental life, though emanating from the material life of society, turns back to it and absorbs it whole. The materialists do not decide: they waver between the two. They affirm dialectical progression in the abstract, but their concrete studies are mostly limited to timeworn explanations along the lines of Hippolyte Taine in terms of 'milieu' and 'moment'.[10]

There is more—beginning with the question, what precisely is this concept of matter the dialecticians use? If they borrow it from science, then it will be the poorest concept that will merge into other concepts to arrive at a concrete notion, the richest one. This notion will, in the end, include the concept of matter within it as one of its structures; but it will not be that concept that explains the notion but, rather, the notion that explains the concept. In this case, it is acceptable to start out from matter as the emptiest of abstractions. It is acceptable also to start out from

10 Except that they define the milieu more precisely as the mode of material life.

being, as Hegel does. The difference is not great, though the Hegelian starting-point, being the more abstract, is the better choice. But if we really have to invert the Hegelian dialectic and 'set it back on its feet', we must admit that matter, chosen as the starting point of the dialectical movement, does not appear to Marxists as the poorest concept but the richest notion. It is identified with the entire universe; it is the unity of all phenomena. Thoughts, life and individuals are merely modes of matter; it is, in short, the great Spinozist totality. Yet, if this is the case, and if Marxist matter is the exact counterpart of Hegelian spirit, we arrive at the paradoxical outcome that Marxism, in order to set the dialectic back on its feet, has put the richest notion at the beginning. And doubtless, for Hegel, Spirit comes at the beginning, but it does so as virtuality, as summons: the dialectic is merely identical with its history. For Marxists, by contrast, it is the whole of matter in action that is given at the outset, and the dialectic, whether it applies to the history of species or to the evolution of human societies, is only ever the retracing of the partial becoming of one of the modes of that reality. But if the dialectic is not, then, the very generation of the world, if it is not progressive enrichment, it is nothing. In obligingly taking up dialectics once again, Marxism has dealt it a death blow. It has unthinkingly killed it with kindness. How, you will ask, has this gone unnoticed? It is because our materialists have built up a slippery, contradictory concept of 'matter'. At times it is the poorest abstraction and at others, the richest concrete totality; as the need dictates. They jump from the one to the other and conceal the one behind the other. And when, finally, you run them to ground and they have no escape, they declare that materialism is a method, an orientation of mind; if you pushed them a little, they would say it was a style of life. They would not be so wrong in this and, for my part, I would be happy to regard it as one of the forms of the esprit de sérieux and the flight from oneself.[11] If materialism is a human attitude, with all that that entails in terms of subjectivity, contradictoriness and sentimentality, then it should not be presented to us as a rigorous philosophy, as the doctrine of objectivity.

I have seen conversions to materialism. It is something taken up as others might take up religion. I would happily define it as the subjectivity of those ashamed of their subjectivity. It is also, of course, the ill-humour of those who suffer in their bodies and know the reality of hunger, illness, manual labour and everything that can sap a human being's vigour. In a word, it is a doctrine of first resort. Now, the first resort is perfectly legitimate, especially when it expresses the

---

11 The esprit de sérieux is one of the two forms of flight from freedom which Sartre identifies in *Being and Nothingness* ([1943] 1956). [Trans.]

spontaneous reaction of oppressed people to their situation—but that does not make it the right one. It always contains a truth, but it goes beyond that truth. To assert, against idealism, the crushing reality of the material world, is not necessarily to be a materialist. We shall come back to this point.

But how does it come about that, in falling from heaven to earth, dialectics retained its necessity? Hegelian consciousness has no need to advance the dialectical hypothesis. It is not a pure objective witness watching the generation of ideas from outside. It is itself dialectical; it engenders itself by the laws of synthetic progression. There is no need at all for it to presuppose necessity in connections; it is that necessity, it lives it. And its certainty does not come to it from some evidence more or less open to criticism, but from the progressive identification of the dialectic of consciousness with the consciousness of the dialectic. If, on the other hand, the dialectic represents the mode of development of the material world, if consciousness, rather than being wholly identified with the entire dialectic, is merely a 'reflection of being', a partial product, a moment of synthetic progress, if, instead of watching its own generation from within, it is invaded from outside by feelings and ideologies that have their roots elsewhere, which it suffers passively without producing them, then it is merely a link in a chain whose beginning and end are very far apart.

And what can it say about the chain that is certain unless it is itself the whole of the chain? The dialectic deposits a few effects in it and carries on its way; considering these effects, thought may judge that they attest to the probable existence of a synthetic mode of progression. Or, alternatively, it may form conjectures on the consideration of external phenomena: in any event, it will have to content itself with regarding the dialectic as a working hypothesis, as a method that must be tried and of which success will be the test. How does it come about that materialists regard this research method as a structure of the universe; how does it come about that they avow themselves certain that the 'interconnection and interdependence of phenomena as established by the dialectical method, are a law of the development of moving matter',[12] since the sciences of nature proceed in a spirit contrary to this and use strictly opposite methods, and since historical science is only at its first tentative beginnings? It is clearly the case that, in transporting the dialectic from one world to the other, they did not wish to forego the advantages it had in the first world. They retained the dialectic's necessity and certainty, while actually giving up such means as they had of verifying them. They wished to give matter the mode of synthetic development that belongs to the idea alone, and

---

12 Stalin, *Dialectical and Historical Materialism*, p. 15.

they borrowed from the idea's reflection in itself a type of certainty that has no place in the experience of the world. But, as a result, matter itself becomes idea: it nominally retains its opacity, inertia and externality, but it offers also a perfect translucency, since its internal processes can be decided on principle and with total certainty; it is a synthesis, it progresses by constant enrichment.

Let us be clear about this; there is no simultaneous transcendence of materialism and idealism here.[13] Opacity and transparency, externality and interiority, inertia and synthetic progression are merely juxtaposed in the spurious unity of 'dialectical materialism'. Matter has remained the matter that science reveals to us. There has been no combination of opposites, for want of a new concept that would really merge them into itself and that would be neither precisely matter nor idea. It is not by surreptitiously attributing the

---

13 Though Marx did sometimes claim there was. In 1844, he wrote that the antinomy between idealism and materialism had to be overcome. And Henri Lefebvre, commenting on his thought, declares in *Le Matérialisme dialectique* (1962), 'Historical materialism, clearly expressed in *Deutsche Ideologie*, achieves the unity of idealism and materialism prefigured and announced in the "1844 Manuscripts"' (pp. 53–4). But then why does M. Garaudy, another spokesman for Marxism, write in *Les Lettres françaises*, 'Sartre rejects materialism and yet claims to avoid idealism. The futility of an impossible "third way" here stands revealed . . . '? What confusion there is in these minds!

qualities of the one to the other that their opposition can be surmounted. It must, in fact, be admitted that, in claiming to be dialectical, materialism 'goes over into' idealism. Just as Marxists claim to be positivists and wreck their positivism by the use they implicitly make of metaphysics, just as they proclaim their rationalism and wreck it by their conception of the origin of thought, so they deny their principle—materialism—in the very moment that they posit it, by a furtive recourse to idealism.[14]

This confusion is reflected in the materialist's subjective attitude to his own doctrine. 'Materialism holds

---

14 It will perhaps be objected that I have not spoken of the common source of all the transformations of the universe, namely energy; that I have taken my stand on the ground of mechanicalism to evaluate dynamistic materialism. My reply is that energy is not a directly perceived reality but a concept forged in order to account for certain phenomena; that scientists know it by its effects rather than by its nature and that, at most, they know, as Poincaré said, that 'something remains'. Besides, the little we can say about it is in strict opposition to the requirements of dialectical materialism: its total quantity is conserved; it is transmitted in discrete quantities; it undergoes a constant degradation. This last principle, in particular, is incompatible with the requirements of a dialectic that claims to enrich itself at each new stage. And let us not forget that a body always receives its energy from without (even intra-atomic energy is received): it is within the framework of the general principle of inertia that the problems of equivalence of energy can be studied. To make energy the vehicle of the dialectic would be to transform it by violence into idea.

that . . . ,' says Stalin. But why does it hold this? Why hold that God does not exist, that mind is a reflection of matter, that the development of the world is a product of contrary forces, that there is an objective truth, that there are no unknowables in the world but only things as yet unknown? We are not told. Only, if it is true that, 'arising out of the new tasks set by the development of the material life of society, new social ideas and theories force their way through, become the possession of the masses, mobilize and organize them against the moribund forces of society, and thus facilitate the overthrow of these forces, which hamper the development of the material life of society',[15] then it seems clear that these ideas are adopted by the proletariat because they account for its present situation and needs, because they are the most effective instrument in its struggle against the bourgeois class. 'The fall of the utopians, including the Narodniks, anarchists and Socialist-Revolutionaries, was due, among other things,' writes Stalin in this same work, to the fact that they did not recognize the primary role which the conditions of the material life of society play in the development of society, and, sinking to idealism, did not base their practical activities on the needs of the development of the material life of society, but, independently and in spite of these needs, on 'ideal plans' and 'all-embracing projects', divorced from the real life of society. The strength

---

15 Stalin, *Dialectical and Historical Materialism*, p. 23.

and vitality of Marxism–Leninism lies in the fact that it does base its practical activity on the needs of the development of the material life of society and never divorces itself from the real life of society.[16]

Though materialism may be the best instrument for action, its truth is pragmatic in nature: it is true for the working class because it works for them. And, since social progress must be made by the working class, it is truer than idealism, which for a time served the interests of the bourgeoisie when it was the rising class and cannot but hamper the development of the material life of society today. But when the proletariat has finally absorbed the bourgeois class into itself and brought about the classless society, new tasks will appear from which new ideas and social theories will 'arise': materialism will have had its day, since it is the thought of the working class and there will no longer be a working class. Grasped objectively and as the expression of the needs and tasks of a class, materialism becomes an opinion. In other words, it is a force of mobilization, transformation and organization, the objective reality of which can be gauged by its power of action. And this opinion that passes itself off as a certitude carries within it its own destruction since, on the basis of its own principles, it must regard itself as objective fact, as reflection of being and as object

16 Stalin, *Dialectical and Historical Materialism*, pp. 21–2.

of science, yet at the same time it destroys the science that must analyse and establish it—at least as opinion. The reasoning is clearly circular and the whole system remains up in the air, perpetually hovering between being and nothingness.

The Stalinist gets out of all this by faith. If he 'holds that' materialism is true, it is because he wants to act and change the world. When you are engaged in such a vast undertaking, you don't have time to quibble over the choice of principles justifying it. He believes in Marx, Lenin and Stalin; he accepts the principle of authority and, lastly, he retains the blind, calm faith that materialism is a certainty. This conviction will colour his general attitude to all the ideas proposed to him. Examine one of his doctrines or concrete assertions at all closely and he will tell you he has no time to lose, that the situation is urgent, that he must first act, deal with the most pressing matters and work for the Revolution. There will be time later on to question principles—or, rather, they will question themselves. For the moment, however, all challenges to his thinking have to be rejected, as they have a weakening effect. This is all very well, but when, in his turn, he attacks or criticizes bourgeois thought or some intellectual position he regards as reactionary, then he claims to hold the truth. The same principles, which a few moments ago he told you it was not quite the time to dispute, suddenly become solid facts. They shift from the level of useful opinions to truths. 'The Trotskyites,' you say to him, 'are wrong; but they aren't police informers, as you claim. You know perfectly well that they aren't.' 'On the contrary,' he will reply, 'I absolutely know that they are. Ultimately what they think is a matter of indifference. Subjectivity doesn't exist. But objectively they are playing the bourgeoisie's game; they are behaving like provocateurs and informers, since unconsciously playing into the hands of the police and deliberately collaborating with them amount to the same thing.' You reply that this is precisely the point: they are not the same thing and, in all objectivity, the behaviour of the Trotskyite and the police officer are not alike. He retorts that the one is as harmful as the other and the effect of both is to retard the advance of the working class. And if you keep at him, if you show him there are many ways of slowing that advance and they are not all equivalent even in their effects, he replies haughtily that these distinctions, even if true, do not interest him. We are in a period of struggle. The situation is simple and the positions clear-cut. Why complicate matters? The Communist militant shouldn't bother his head about these nuances. And we are back once more with pragmatism, so that the proposition 'the Trotskyite is an informer' wavers perpetually between the status of useful opinion and objective truth.[17]

---

17 Here I am summarizing conversations on Trotskyism I have had on many occasions with Communist intellectuals—and

Nothing demonstrates the ambiguity of the Marxist notion of truth better than the ambivalence in the Communist attitude to scientists. The Communists appeal to scientists, exploit their discoveries and present their thinking as the only type of valid knowledge. Yet they never lower their guard towards them. Insofar as they base themselves on the rigorous notion of objectivity, they need the scientists' critical spirit, their taste for research and for attacking established opinion, their clearsightedness, which rejects authority and reverts always to experiment or rational proof. But they are distrustful of these same virtues inasmuch as they are believers and inasmuch as science calls all beliefs into question. If the scientist brings his scientific qualities to the party, if he claims the right to examine principles, he becomes an 'intellectual' and his dangerous freedom of thought, an expression of his relative material independence, finds itself opposed by the faith of the militant worker who, by his very situation, needs to believe in the directives of his leaders.[18]

This, then, is the materialism for which they want me to opt: a monster, an elusive Proteus, a great vague,

---

not the least significant of them. In every case, they have taken the course I indicate.

18 Ultimately, as we see in the Lysenko affair, the scientist who gave Marxist politics its foundations by providing materialism with its guarantees must now submit in his research to the exigencies of that politics. This is a vicious circle.

contradictory sham. They ask me to choose, this very day, in all freedom and all lucidity, and what I must choose freely and lucidly, with the best of my thought, is a doctrine that destroys thought. I know there is no other salvation for humanity than the liberation of the working class: I know this before being a materialist and on the simple inspection of the facts. I know the interests of the mind lie with the proletariat: is that any reason for me to demand of my thought, which brought me to this point, that it destroy itself? Is it any reason to force it now to relinquish its criteria, to embrace self-contradiction, to be torn between incompatible arguments, to lose even the clear consciousness of itself, to launch forth blindly on a giddy race towards faith? 'Get down on your knees and you will believe,' says Pascal. What the materialist does is very similar to this.

Now, if it were just a matter of me getting down on my knees and if, by that sacrifice, I could ensure humanity's happiness, I would no doubt consent to do so. But it is actually a question of giving up everyone's entitlement to free criticism, to facts and, in a word, to truth. I am told we shall get these things back later. But there is no proof this is the case. How could I believe in a promise made in the name of self-destroying principles? I know only one thing: my mind has, this very day, to throw in the towel. Have I fallen into this unacceptable dilemma: to betray the proletariat in order to serve truth or to betray truth in the name of the proletariat?

If I consider the materialist faith not in terms of its content but of its history, as a social phenomenon, I can clearly see it is not a whim of intellectuals nor a mere error on the part of a philosopher. As far back as I go, I find it associated with the revolutionary attitude. Epicurus, the first man actually to try to free men from their fears and their chains, the first man to try to abolish slavery on his land, was a materialist. The materialism of the great philosophers—and, indeed, that of the 'sociétés de pensée'—played no small part in paving the way for the French Revolution. And, lastly, using an argument very closely akin to that used by Catholics in defending their faith, the Communists are fond of arguing that, 'if materialism were wrong, how do you explain how it has united the working class, enabled them to be led into battle, and brought us, despite the most violent repression, this succession of victories in the last half century?' This argument, which is a scholastic one, of proof a posteriori by success, is not insignificant.

It has to be said that materialism is today the philosophy of the proletariat, precisely insofar as the proletariat is revolutionary. This austere, mendacious doctrine is the bearer of the purest, most ardent hopes; this theory which denies human freedom root and branch has become the instrument of humanity's most thoroughgoing liberation. This indicates that its content is suited to 'mobilizing and organizing' revolutionary forces; and that there is a deep connection between the situation of an oppressed class and the materialist expression of that situation. But we cannot conclude from this that materialism is a philosophy or, still less, that it is the truth.

Insofar as it enables coherent action to be mounted, insofar as it expresses a concrete situation, insofar as millions of people find hope and an image of their condition in it, materialism must undoubtedly contain some truth. But this in no sense means that it is wholly true as a doctrine. The truths it contains may be shrouded and drowned in error; it may be that, in order to cope with the urgent tasks before it, revolutionary thinking has thrown up a rapid, temporary construction for getting to those truths, has developed what dressmakers call a basted garment. In that case, there is much more in materialism than the revolutionary requires. There is also much less, for this hasty, forced tacking-together of truths prevents them from acquiring a spontaneous structure among themselves and attaining their true unity. Materialism is indisputably the only myth that fits with revolutionary exigencies, and the politician looks no further. The myth serves him, he adopts it. But if his undertaking is to stand the test of time, it is not a myth he needs but the Truth. It is the philosopher's business to make the truths contained in materialism hold together and, little by little, to constitute a philosophy that suits revolutionary exigencies as exactly as the myth does. And the best means for identifying these truths within the error in which they are immersed is to determine those exigencies from an attentive examination of the revolutionary attitude; to retrace, in each case, the path by which they have given rise to the call for a materialist representation of the universe; and to see whether they have not, each time, been deflected and diverted from their initial meaning. Perhaps if they are freed from the myth that both crushes them and conceals them from themselves, they will yield the broad lineaments of a coherent philosophy that has the advantage over materialism of being a true description of nature and human relations.

The Nazis and their collaborators proceeded by blurring ideas. The Pétain regime called itself a Revolution, and things reached such a point of absurdity that one day La Gerbe ran the following headline: 'Conserve!—this is the motto of the National Revolution'. It is right, then, that we recall here a number of elementary truths. To avoid any presuppositions, we shall adopt the a posteriori definition given by historian Albert Mathiez: in his view, a revolution occurs when a change in institutions is accompanied by a profound modification of the regime of ownership.

We shall term that party or person within a party revolutionary whose acts intentionally work towards such a revolution. And the first thing we have to say is that not everyone can become a revolutionary. Doubtless, the existence of a strong, organized party with revolutionary aims may exert its attraction on individuals or groups of all origins, but the organization of that party can be the work only of persons of a determinate social condition. In other words, revolutionaries are in situation. They are clearly to be found only among the oppressed, but being oppressed is not enough to make one desire to be a revolutionary. We may class the Jews among the oppressed—and the same holds true in some countries for ethnic minorities—but many of them are oppressed within the bourgeoisie and, as they share the privileges of the class that oppresses them, they cannot without contradiction work towards the destruction of those privileges. In the same way, we cannot term the feudal nationalists of the colonies revolutionary, nor the American blacks, even though their interests may coincide with those of the party working towards revolution: the integration of these groups into society is not complete. What the former call for is the return to an earlier state of affairs: they wish to recover their supremacy and break the ties that bind them to the colonial society. What American blacks and bourgeois Jews want is equal rights, which in no way implies a structural change in the regime of property rights. They merely wish to share in the privileges of their oppressors, which is to say that they are, ultimately, seeking a more complete integration.

Revolutionaries are in a situation where they cannot in any sense share in these privileges. It is by the destruction of the class oppressing them that they can obtain their demands. This means that their oppression is not, like that of the Jews or the American Negroes, a secondary and, as it were, lateral characteristic of the social regime in question but that it is, in fact, constitutive. Revolutionaries are, therefore, both oppressed persons and the keystone of the society oppressing them. To put it more plainly, it is as an oppressed person that the revolutionary is indispensable to that society. That is to say, the revolutionary is one of those who work for the dominant class.

Revolutionaries are necessarily oppressed persons and workers, and it is as workers that they are oppressed. This dual character of producer and oppressed indi- vidual suffices to define the situation of revolutionaries, but not the revolutionaries themselves. The canuts of Lyon or the workers of the 1848 'June days' were not revolutionaries, but rioters. They were fighting for a particular improvement of their lot, not for its radical transformation. This means their situation was confined to themselves alone and, taken overall, they accepted it: they accepted being wage workers and working on machines they did not own; they acknowledged the rights of the owners and obeyed the morality of that class. It was simply the case that, within a set of circumstances they had neither transcended nor even recognized, they were calling for an increase in wages.

Revolutionaries, by contrast, are defined by the transcendence of the situation in which they find themselves. And because they go beyond that situation in the direction of a radically new one, they can grasp it as a synthetic whole or, to put it another way, they make it exist for them as a totality. It is on the basis of this transcendence towards the future, then, and from the standpoint of the future, that they realize that situation. Instead of appearing to them, as it does to the resigned victims of oppression, as a definitive, a priori structure, it is for them only one moment of the universe. Since they wish to change it, since they view it at the very outset from the standpoint of history, they regard themselves as historical agents.

From the very beginning, then, by this self-projection into the future, they escape the society that is crushing them and gain a vantage point that enables them to understand it: they see a human history at one with human destiny, a history in which the change they wish to effect is, if not the goal, then at least an essential step on the way. History appears to them as progress, since they consider the state they wish to lead us to as better than the one in which we currently find ourselves. At the same time they see human relations from the viewpoint of work, since work is their lot. Now, work is, among other things, a direct connection between human beings and the universe: it is humanity's purchase on nature and, at the same time, a primordial type of relationship between human beings. It is, therefore, an essential attitude of human reality which, in the unity of a single project, both 'exists' and makes exist, in their mutual dependence, its relation to nature and its relation to others. And, insofar as they call for their liberation as workers, they know very well that this cannot come about by their mere integration into the privileged class. Rather, what they wish is for the relations of solidarity they maintain with other workers to become the very model of human relations. They wish, therefore, for the liberation of the oppressed class in its entirety. Unlike the rebel, who stands alone, the revolutionaries' self-understanding requires relations of solidarity with their class.

Thus, because they are aware of the social structure on which they depend, revolutionaries demand a philosophy that takes account of their situation and, since their action has no meaning unless it involves the fate of all humanity, that philosophy has to be total: that is to say, it has to provide a total elucidation of the human condition. And since they are themselves, as workers, an essential structure of society and the hinge between human beings and nature, they can have no truck with a philosophy that would not primarily and centrally express the original relationship of man to the world, which is, precisely, the coordinated action of the one on the other. Lastly, since this philosophy arises out of a historical enterprise and has to represent for the person requiring it a certain mode of historicization which that person has chosen, it necessarily has to present the course of history as oriented or, at least, as capable of orientation. And since it arises out of action and focuses back on action, which requires it for its elucidation, it is not a contemplation of the world but must itself be an action. Let us be clear that it is not something super-added to the revolutionary effort; it is indistinguishable from that effort. It is contained in the original project of the worker who joins the party of revolution, since any project to change the world is inseparable from a certain understanding which discloses the world from the standpoint of the change in it that one is trying to bring about. The revolutionary philosopher's task will consist, then, in identifying and making explicit the great guiding themes of the revolutionary attitude, and that philosophical task is itself an act, since the philosopher can identify those themes only if he situates himself within the movement engendering them: namely, the revolutionary movement. It is also an act because, once this philosophy is made explicit, it renders the militant more conscious of his destiny, his place in the world and his goals.

So revolutionary thinking is a thinking in situation: it is the thinking of the oppressed insofar as they rise up together against oppression. It cannot be reconstructed from outside. It can merely be learned, once it has been developed, by reproducing in oneself the revolutionary movement and viewing it from the standpoint of the situation from which it emanates. We should note that the thinking of philosophers from the ruling class also constitutes action, as Nizan has clearly shown in his book, Les Chiens de garde.[19] Its aim is to defend, conserve and repel. But its inferiority to revolutionary thinking comes from the fact that the philosophy of oppression seeks to hide its pragmatic character from itself. Since it aims not to change the world, but to keep it in being, it claims to contemplate the world as it is. It views society and nature from the standpoint of pure knowledge, without admitting to itself that this attitude tends to perpetuate the present state of the world by convincing us that it is easier to know it than to change it or, at least, that if we want to change it, we must first know it.

The theory of the primacy of knowledge exerts a negative, inhibiting effect by conferring a pure, static essence on things, unlike any philosophy of work which grasps the object through the action that modifies that object by using it. But it contains in itself a negation of the effect it exerts, since, precisely, it asserts the primacy of knowing and rejects any pragmatic conception of truth. The superiority of revolutionary thinking lies in the fact that it proclaims its character as action from the outset; it is conscious of being an act; and if it presents itself as a total understanding of the universe, that is because the project of

19 Paul Nizan, *The Watchdogs: Philosophers and the Established Order* (New York: Monthly Review Press, 1972).

the oppressed worker is a total attitude towards the universe as a whole. But since revolutionaries need to distinguish the true from the false, this indissoluble unity of thought and action calls for a new and systematic theory of truth. The pragmatic conception cannot meet their requirements, since it is subjectivist idealism pure and simple. This is why the materialist myth was invented. It has the advantage of reducing thought to being merely one of the forms of universal energy and thus divesting it of its wan, will-o'-the-wisp aspect. Moreover, it presents thought in each case as one objective behaviour among others; in other words, as something brought about by the state of the world and reacting back on that state to modify it. But we have just seen that the notion of a conditioned thinking collapses of itself; further on, I shall demonstrate that the same applies to the notion of determinate action. The point is not to create a cosmogonic myth to give symbolic representation to the act of thought, but to abandon all myths and return to the true revolutionary requirement which is that of uniting action and truth, thought and realism. In a word, we need a philosophical theory which shows that human reality is action and that action on the world is the same as the understanding of that world as it is; which shows, in other words, that action is disclosure of reality at the same time as it is modification of that reality.[20] But, as we have seen, the materialist myth is, additionally, the figurative representation, within the unity of a cosmology, of the movement of history, of the relation of human beings to matter and the relation of human beings among themselves. It is, in short, the figurative representation of all the revolutionary themes. We must go back, then, to the structuring of the revolutionary attitude and examine it in detail to see whether it calls only for a mythic figuration or whether, by contrast, it calls for the groundwork of a rigorous philosophy.

Every member of the dominant class is a man of divine right. Born into a world of leaders, he is convinced from childhood that he is born to command and, in a sense, this is true because his parents have bred him to take over from them. There is a certain social function that awaits him in the future, a function into which he will slip as soon as he is old enough and which is akin to the metaphysical reality of his person. In his own eyes, then, he is a person, an a priori synthesis of fact and legal right. Awaited by his peers and destined to take over from them in due course, he exists because he has the right to exist. This sacred character of one bourgeois for another, which manifests itself in ceremonies of recognition (such as

---

20 This is what Marx, in *Theses on Feuerbach* (1924), calls 'practical materialism'. But why materialism?

greetings, visiting cards, formal announcements, ritual visits, etc.), is what is called human dignity. The ideology of the ruling class is steeped in this idea of dignity. And when men are said to be 'the lords of creation', this should be understood in its most literal form: they are its divine-right monarchs; the world is made for them; their existence is the absolute value, perfectly satisfying to the mind, that gives the universe its meaning. This is what is originally meant in all the philosophical systems that assert the primacy of subject over object and the constitution of nature by the activity of thought. It is self-evident that, in these conditions, man is a supernatural being. What is called nature is the sum total of what exists without having the right to do so.

For the sacred individuals, the oppressed classes are part of nature. They must not command. Perhaps in other societies the fact of a slave's being born within the domus conferred a sacred character on him also: that of being born to serve; of being, over against the man of divine right, the man of divine duty. But in the case of the proletariat the same cannot be said. The worker's son, born in some outlying industrial district, living among the crowd, has no direct contact with the propertied elite. He has no personal duties other than those laid down by the law; he is not even forbidden, if he possesses that mysterious grace known as merit, to gain access, under certain circumstances and on certain conditions, to the upper class, at which point his son or grandson will become a man by divine right. In this way, he is simply a living being, the best organized of the animals. Everyone has felt the contempt implicit in the term 'natural' that is used to refer to the natives of a colonial land. The banker, the industrialist or even the teacher from the 'home country' are not the 'natural' inhabitants of any country; they do not fall into this natural category at all. By contrast, the oppressed person does: each of the events in his life tells him he is not entitled to exist. His parents did not bring him into the world for any particular end, but by chance and for nothing. At best, it was because they loved children or because they were susceptible to a certain kind of propaganda or because they wanted to enjoy the benefits granted to large families. No special function awaits him; and if he is apprenticed, this is not to prepare him to exercise the priesthood of a profession but merely to enable him to prolong the unjustifiable existence he has been leading since his birth. He will work in order to live, and to say the ownership of the fruits of his labour will be stolen from him is an understatement: the very meaning of his work is stolen from him, since he feels himself no part of the society for which he produces.

Whether he is a fitter or a labourer, he knows very well that he is not irreplaceable. Indeed, it is this interchangeability that characterizes the 'workers'. The work of the doctor or the lawyer is judged by its quality, that of the 'good' worker by its quantity alone. Through the circumstances of his situation he becomes aware of himself as a member of a zoological species: the human species. So long as he remains on this level, his condition itself seems natural to him: he will carry on his life as he began it, with sudden revolts if oppression bears down on him more strongly, but these will be merely spontaneous.

The revolutionary transcends this situation because he wants to change it. And it is from the point of view of this will-to-change that he regards it. We must note, first of all, that he wants to change it for his whole class, not for himself. If he were thinking merely of himself he could, as we have seen, leave the terrain of the species and embrace the values of the dominant class. Self-evidently in that case he would accept a priori the sacred character of the men of divine right, for the sole purpose of benefitting from it in his turn. But, as he cannot envisage claiming that divine right for his whole class, since it originates precisely in an oppression he wishes to destroy, his first move will be to contest the rights of the ruling class. In his eyes, the men of divine right do not exist. He has not moved among them, but he senses that they lead an existence not unlike his own, equally vague and unjustifiable. Unlike the members of the oppressor class, he does not seek to exclude the members of the other class from the human community. But he wants, from the outset, to divest them of that magical aspect that makes them formidable for those whom they oppress. Moreover, a spontaneous impulse leads him to deny the values they have initially established. If it were true that theirs was an a priori Good, then revolution would be poisoned in its essence: to rise up against the oppressor class would be to rise up against Good in general. But his plan is not to replace this Good by another a priori Good, for he is not in the phase of construction: he merely wishes to free himself from all the values and rules of conduct the ruling class has devised because those values and rules are simply a brake on his activity and are, by their very nature, aimed at preserving the status quo. And since he wishes to change the way society is organized, he has first to reject the idea that it was ordained by Providence: only if he regards it as a fact can he hope to replace it with another fact that suits him better.

At the same time, revolutionary thought is humanistic. The assertion that 'we too are human beings' underlies all revolutions. And, by this, the revolutionary means that his oppressors are human beings. He will, no doubt, do violence to them; he will attempt to throw off their yoke but, if he must destroy some of their lives, he will always try to keep this destruction to a minimum because he needs technicians and managers. So even the bloodiest of revolutions involves defections; it is, above all, an absorption and assimilation of the oppressor class by the oppressed class. By contrast with the turncoats or members of a persecuted minority who want to raise themselves to the level of the privileged and assimilate to them, revolutionaries want to bring them down to their level by denying the validity of their privileges. And, since the continual sense of their contingency inclines them to recognize themselves as unjustifiable facts, they regard the men of divine right as mere facts similar to themselves. Revolutionaries are not, then, people who claim rights but, rather, people who destroy the very notion of right, which they see as a product of custom and force. Their humanism is not based on human dignity, but denies human beings any particular dignity; the unity in which they wish to merge all their fellows and themselves is not that of the human realm, but of the human species. There is a human species, an unjustifiable, contingent phenomenon; the circumstances of its development have brought it to a kind of inner imbalance; the revolutionary's task is to make it find a more rational equilibrium beyond its present state. Just as the species has closed around the men of divine right and absorbed them, so nature closes around human beings and absorbs them: the human being is a natural fact; humanity is one species among others.

Only in this way does the revolutionary think he can escape the mystifications of the privileged class.

The man who knows himself to be natural can never again be mystified by the recourse to a priori moralities. At this point materialism seems to offer him its aid; it is the epic of the factual. The links that form across the materialist world are no doubt necessary, but necessity appears here within an original contingency. If the universe exists, its development and successive states may be governed by laws. But it is not a necessity that the universe should exist, or that there should be Being in general, and the contingency of the universe communicates itself through all the connections—even the most rigorous ones—to each particular fact. Each state, governed from outside by the previous one, may be modified if one acts on its causes. And the new state is neither more nor less natural than the preceding one, if by this we mean that it is not based on rights and that its necessity is merely relative. At the same time, since it is a question of imprisoning man in the world, materialism possesses the advantage of offering a crude myth of the origin of species in which the most complex forms derive from the simplest. It is not a matter of replacing the end by the cause in each case, but of presenting a stereotyped image of a world in which causes have everywhere replaced ends. That materialism has always had this function can already be seen in the attitude of the first and most naive of the great materialists: Epicurus recognizes that an endless number of different explanations could be as true as materialism. That is to say, they could account for the phenomena just as exactly. But he defies us to find one that frees man from his fears more completely. And the essential fear of human beings, particularly where they are suffering, is not so much death or the existence of a harsh God, but simply that the state of affairs from which they are suffering was produced and is maintained for unknowable, transcendent ends. Any effort to modify it would then be futile and blameworthy. A subtle discouragement would insinuate itself right into their judgements and prevent them from wishing for, or even conceiving of, any improvement. Epicurus reduced death to a fact by removing from it the moral aspect it gained from the fiction of underworld seats of judgement. He did not eliminate ghosts, but he turned them into strictly physical phenomena. He did not dare eliminate the gods, but he reduced them to being merely a divine species unrelated to ourselves. He took from them the power to create themselves and showed they were produced, as we are, by the streaming of atoms.

But here again, though it may have been useful and encouraging, is the materialist myth really necessary? What the consciousness of the revolutionary demands is that the privileges of the oppressor class should be unjustifiable, that the original contingency he finds within himself should also be constitutive of the very existence of his oppressors and, lastly, that the system of values constructed by his masters, the aim of which is to confer a de jure existence on de facto advantages, can be supplanted by an as yet non-existent form of organization of the world that will exclude all privileges de jure and de facto. But he clearly has an ambivalent attitude to the natural. In a way, he plunges into nature, dragging his masters with him, but, on the other hand, he declares that he wishes to substitute a rational scheme of human relations for the combination blindly produced by nature.

The expression Marxism uses to refer to the future society is antiphysis. This means that the aim is to establish a human order whose laws will be the negation of natural laws. And doubtless we are meant to understand that this order will be produced only by first obeying the prescriptions of nature. But, ultimately, the fact is that this order must be conceived within the nature that denies it; the fact is that, in the anti-natural society, the representation of the law will precede the establishment of the law, instead of the law conditioning the representation we have of it, as, according to materialism, it does today.

In short, the transition to antiphysis signifies the replacement of the society of laws by the community of ends. And, without a doubt, the revolutionary distrusts values and refuses to acknowledge that he is pursuing a better organization of the human community:

he fears that a return to values, even by a detour, may open the door to new mystifications. But, on the other hand, the mere fact that he is willing to sacrifice his life for an order that he never expects to see arrive implies that that future order, which justifies all his acts but which he will not enjoy, functions for him as a value. What is a value if not the call of that which does not yet exist?[21]

In order to meet these various demands, a revolutionary philosophy should set aside the materialist myth and attempt to show: (1) that man is unjustifiable; that his existence is contingent insofar as neither he nor any Providence has produced it; (2) in consequence, that any collective order established by human beings may be transcended in the direction of other orders; (3) that the value system in force in a society reflects the structure of that society and tends to preserve it; (4) that it may, therefore, always be transcended in the direction of other systems, which are not clearly perceived, since the society they will express does not exist yet, but are foreshadowed and, all in all, invented by the very efforts of the members of the society to transcend that society. The oppressed

---

21 This same ambiguity can be found in the judgements passed by Communists on their opponents. For, after all, materialism should prevent them from making judgements: a bourgeois is merely the product of a rigorous necessity. Yet the entire tone of L'Humanité is one of moral indignation.

person lives out his original contingency, and revolutionary philosophy must take account of this. But, in living out his contingency, he accepts the right to existence of his oppressors and the absolute value of the ideologies they have produced. He becomes a revolutionary only by a movement of transcendence that throws those rights and ideologies into question.

Revolutionary philosophy has, above all, to explain the possibility of this movement of transcendence. It is clear that it cannot derive its source from the purely material, natural existence of the individual, since it looks back over that existence to judge it from the standpoint of the future. This possibility of rising above a situation to gain a vantage point on it (a vantage point that is not pure knowledge but is, inseparably, both understanding and action) is precisely what we call freedom. No kind of materialism will ever explain it. A sequence of causes and effects may well induce from me an action or a course of behaviour which will itself be an effect and will modify the state of the world. It cannot make me look back on my situation to grasp it in its totality. In a word, it cannot account for revolutionary class consciousness. The materialist dialectic is no doubt there to explain and justify this transcendence in the direction of the future. But it works to lodge freedom in things, not in human beings, which is absurd. A state of the world will never be able to produce class consciousness.

Marxists know this so well that they rely on militants—that is to say on conscious, concerted action—to radicalize the masses and arouse this consciousness in them. This is all very well, but where do these militants find their understanding of the situation? Must they not, at some point or other, have risen above the situation, or stepped back from it? Lastly, to avoid the revolutionary's being mystified by his former masters, he has to be shown that established values are mere facts. But if they are facts and, as a result, capable of being transcended, this is not because they are values but because they are something established. And to avoid his mystifying himself, he has to be given the means of understanding that the goal he is pursuing—whether he calls it antiphysis, the classless society or the liberation of man—is also a value; and if there is no way of going beyond this value, that is only because it has not yet been realized. This is what Marx sensed when he spoke of going beyond Communism, and Trotsky when he talked of permanent revolution. A contingent, unjustifiable, but free being, wholly immersed in a society that oppresses him, but capable of transcending that society by his efforts to change it—this is what the revolutionary human being demands to be. Idealism mystifies him by tying him up with already established rights and values; it conceals from him his power to invent his own path. But materialism also mystifies him, by robbing him of his freedom. Revolutionary philosophy must be a philosophy of transcendence.

But, all sophistry apart, the revolutionary himself mistrusts freedom. And he is right to do so. There has never been any lack of prophets to tell him he is free, and in each case it was to dupe him. Stoic freedom, Christian freedom and Bergsonian freedom have merely strengthened his chains by concealing them. They were all reducible to a certain inner freedom that human beings could preserve in any situation. This inner freedom is a pure idealist mystification: care is taken not to present it as the necessary condition for action. It is, in fact, pure enjoyment of itself. If Epictetus in chains does not rebel, that is because he feels free, he enjoys his freedom. But on this basis, one state of affairs is as good as another; the slave is as free as the master; why wish for change?

Ultimately, this freedom is reducible to a more or less clear assertion of the autonomy of thought. But in conferring independence on thought, it separates it from the situation (since truth is universal, one may think truth in any situation whatever) and separates it also from action (since the intention alone depends on us, the act, in being performed, undergoes pressure from the world's real forces, which distort it and render it unrecognizable to its very perpetrator). Abstract thoughts and empty intentions are all that are left to the slave in the name of metaphysical freedom. And, meanwhile, his masters' orders or the need to make a living have committed him to harsh, concrete actions, and compel him to form detailed thoughts about matter and tools.

The liberating element for the oppressed individual is, in fact, work. In this sense, it is initially work that is revolutionary. Admittedly, that work is done to order and appears initially as the subjugation of the worker. It is improbable that he would have chosen to do this work in these conditions and in this time span for this pay if he had not been compelled to. More rigorous than the master of ancient times, the employer goes so far as to determine in advance the actions and behaviour of the worker. He breaks down the worker's act into elements, takes some of these away to have them done by other workers and reduces the conscious, synthetic activity to a mere sum of indefinitely repeated movements. In this way, by assimilating the worker's actions to properties, he tends to reduce him to the state of a thing, pure and simple. Mme de Staël cites a striking example of such a reduction in her account of the journey she made to Russia in the early nineteenth century: 'Out of twenty musicians (of a band of Russian serfs), each one plays one single note each time it recurs. As a result, each of these men bears the name of the note he is responsible for sounding. As they go by, one hears, "There is Mr Narishkine's G, E or D".' Here, then, is the individual

limited to a constant property that defines him, like
an atomic weight or a melting point. Modern Taylorism does just this. The worker becomes the man of
a single operation, which he repeats a hundred times
a day. He is merely an object and it would be childish
or despicable to tell a shoe-stitcher or the worker who
puts the needles in the speedometers of Ford cars that,
amid the action they are involved in, they retain their
inner freedom of thought. But at the same time, work
offers the beginnings of a concrete liberation, even in
these extreme cases, because it is, first, the negation of
the contingent, capricious order that is the master's
order. At work, the oppressed individual is no longer
concerned to please the master; he escapes the world
of the dance-band, of politeness, ceremony and psychology; he does not have to guess what is going on
in the boss's head; he is no longer at the mercy of
someone's mood. His work is, admittedly, imposed on
him at the outset and the fruits of his labours are
stolen from him at the end. But within these two limits, his work confers on him a mastery of things; the
worker apprehends himself as the possibility of infinitely varying the form of a material object by acting
upon it in accordance with certain universal rules. In
other words, it is the determinism of matter that offers
him the first image of his freedom.

A worker is not deterministic in the way a scientist
is. He does not subscribe to determinism as an explicitly

formulated postulate. He lives it in his gestures, in the movement of an arm striking a rivet or lowering a lever. He is so steeped in determinism that, when the desired effect is not produced, he will try to find what hidden cause has prevented it from occurring, without ever supposing any waywardness in things or any sudden, contingent breakdown in the natural order. And since it is at the deepest point of his slavery, at the very moment the master's whim transforms him into a thing, that his action liberates him by conferring on him the government of things and a specialist's autonomy the master cannot infringe, the idea of liberation has become combined in his mind with that of determinism. He cannot, in fact, apprehend freedom as something floating above the world, since, for the master or the oppressor class he is, precisely, a thing. He does not learn that he is free by looking back reflexively upon himself but, rather, transcends his slavish state by his action on phenomena which, by the very rigorousness with which they are connected, reflect back to him the image of a concrete freedom: namely, his freedom to modify them. And since the beginnings of his concrete freedom appear to him in the links of determinism, it is no surprise that he aims to replace the relation of man to man, which seems to him the relation of a tyrannical freedom to a humiliated obedience, with a relation of man to thing; and finally, from another standpoint—since the man who governs things is in turn a thing—by a relation of thing to thing.

Hence, determinism—insofar as it stands opposed to the psychology of civility—looks to him like a purifying form of thought, a catharsis. And if he looks back at himself to regard himself as a determinate thing, he thereby liberates himself from the formidable freedom of his masters, as he sweeps them up with him into the connecting links of determinism and regards them in their turn as things, by explaining their orders in terms of their situation, instincts and history—that is, by immersing them in the world. If all men are things, there are no longer any slaves; there are only the de facto oppressed. Like Samson, who consented to be buried beneath the ruins of the temple, provided that the Philistines perished with him, the slave frees himself by eliminating the freedom of his masters with his own and being engulfed, alongside them, in matter. The liberated society of his conceiving is the opposite of Kant's community of ends; it is not based on the reciprocal recognition of freedoms. But, since the liberating relationship is that between man and things, that is what will constitute the basic structure of this society. The relation of oppression between men has merely to be eliminated for the wills of both slave and master, worn down by reciprocal struggle, to be entirely redirected towards things. Liberated society will be a harmonious enterprise of exploitation of the world. As it is produced by the absorption of the privileged classes and is defined by work or, in other words, by action on matter and, as it is itself subject to the laws of determinism, the circle is closed and the world is rounded off once more. Unlike the rebel, the revolutionary wants an order. And since the spiritual orders he is offered are always more or less the mystifying image of the society oppressing him, it is the material order he will choose—that is to say, the order of effectiveness, in which he will figure both as cause and effect. Here again, materialism offers itself. The materialist myth offers the most exact image of a society in which freedoms are alienated.

Auguste Comte defined it as the doctrine that seeks to explain the higher in terms of the lower. Naturally, the terms 'higher' and 'lower' are not to be taken in a moral sense here, but refer to more or less complicated forms of organization. Now, it is precisely the case that the worker is regarded by the person he feeds and protects as an inferior, and the oppressor class takes itself originally for the upper class. By dint of the fact that its internal structures are more complex and refined, it is that class which produces ideologies, culture and value systems. The tendency of the upper strata of society is to explain the lower in terms of the higher, either by regarding the lower as a debasement of the higher or by taking the view that it exists in order to serve the needs of the higher. This type of teleological explanation is, naturally, elevated into a general principle for interpreting the universe. By contrast, the explanation 'from below'—that is to say, in terms of economic, technical and ultimately biological conditioning—is the one the oppressed adopt, because it makes them the foundation of the whole society. If the higher is merely an emanation of the lower, then the 'exquisite class' is merely an epiphenomenon. If the oppressed refuse to serve it, it withers and dies; by itself it is nothing. One has only to expand this—correct—conception and turn it into a general explanatory principle for materialism to be born. And the materialist explanation of the universe—that is, of the biological by the physico-chemical and of thought by matter—becomes in its turn a justification of the revolutionary attitude; by creating a structured myth, this explanation turns a spontaneous stirring of revolt of the oppressed against their oppressor into a universal mode of existence of reality.

Here again, materialism gives the revolutionary more than he asks for. For the revolutionary asks to govern things, not to be one. Admittedly, he has acquired from his work a proper estimation of freedom. The freedom reflected back to him by his action on things is far removed from the Stoic's abstract freedom of thought. It manifests itself in a particular situation, into which the worker has been thrown by the chance of his birth and by the whim or self-interest of his master. It appears within an undertaking that he did not begin of his own free will and that he will not finish; it cannot be distinguished from his very engagement within that undertaking; but ultimately if, in the very depths of his slavery, he becomes aware of his freedom, this is because he can gauge the effectiveness of his concrete action. He does not possess the pure idea of an autonomy that he does not enjoy but he knows his power, which is proportionate to his action. What he finds, during the action itself, is that he transcends the present state of matter through a precise plan for arranging it in a particular way and since that plan is identical with the government-of-means-with-a-view-to-ends, he succeeds in fact in arranging it as he wanted. If he discovers the relation of cause and effect, he does so not by suffering it but in the very act that transcends the present state (the adherence of coal to the walls of the mine, etc.) in the direction of a certain goal that casts light on and, from the depths of the future, defines that state. So the causal relation discloses itself in and through the efficacy of an act that is both project and realization.

It is the tractability and, with it, the resistance of the universe that reflect back to him at one and the same time both the constancy of causal series and the image of his freedom, but that is because his freedom is indistinguishable from the use of causal series for an end that it sets itself. Without the light that end casts on the present situation, there would be neither causal relation nor means–ends relationship in this situation; or, rather, there would be an indistinct infinity of means and ends, effects and causes, the way there would be an undifferentiated infinity of circles, ellipses, triangles and polygons, were it not for the generative act of the mathematician who draws a particular figure by linking a series of points selected in terms of some law. Thus, in the performance of work, determinism does not reveal freedom insofar as it is an abstract law of nature, but only insofar as a human project carves out and throws light on a certain partial determinism amid the infinite interaction of phenomena. And in this determinism, which finds its proof simply in the efficacy of human action—in much the same way as Archimedes' Principle was already in use and understood by shipbuilders long before Archimedes gave it its conceptual form—the relationship of cause to effect is indistinguishable from that of means to end.

The organic unity of the worker's project consists in the simultaneous emergence of an end that was not originally in the universe, which manifests itself through the disposition of means for achieving it (for the end is nothing other than the synthetic unity of all the means brought together to produce it). At the same time, the undergirding for these means, which reveals itself in turn in their very disposition, is the relation of cause and effect: like Archimedes' Principle, which was both the underpinning and the content of the shipbuilders' technique. In this sense, we may say that the atom is created by the atomic bomb, which is conceivable only in the light of the Anglo-American project of winning a war. Thus, freedom is discovered only in the act, is indivisible from the act; it is the foundation of the connections and interactions that form the internal structures of the act; it is never mere self-enjoyment, but reveals itself in and through its products; it is not an inner virtue that gives one licence to detach oneself from the most urgent situations, since, for human beings, there is neither outside nor inside. It is, rather, the power to commit oneself to present action and to build a future; it generates a future that enables us to understand and change the present. So the worker actually learns his freedom through things: but precisely because things teach him his freedom, he is anything but a thing. And it is here that materialism mystifies him and becomes, in spite of itself, an instrument in the hands of the oppressors: for if the worker discovers his freedom in his work, conceived as the original relation of man to material things, he thinks of himself as a thing in his relations with the master who oppresses him; it is the master who, in reducing him through Taylorism or any other procedure, to be merely an ever-identical sum of operations, transforms him into a passive object, the mere medium of constant properties.

Materialism, by breaking man down into units of behaviour conceived strictly along the lines of Taylorist operations, plays the master's game; it is the master who conceives the slave as a machine; by regarding himself as a mere product of nature, as a 'natural being', the slave sees himself through the master's eyes. He conceives himself as an Other and with the thoughts of the Other. There is a unity between the materialist revolutionary's conception and that of his oppressors. Now, doubtless it will be said that the result of materialism is to catch the master and transform him into a thing like the slave. But the master knows nothing of this and cares less: he lives within his ideologies, rights and culture. It is only to the subjectivity of the slave that he appears as a thing. It is, therefore, infinitely more useful and true to allow the slave to discover through his work his freedom to change the world and, consequently, to change his own state, than to go to enormous lengths, by concealing his true freedom from him, to demonstrate to him that his master is a thing. And, if it is true that materialism, as an explanation of the higher by the lower, is an appropriate picture of the current structure of our society, it is simply all the more obvious that this is merely a myth in the Platonic sense of the term. For the revolutionary has no concern for a symbolic expression of the present situation; he wants a form of thought that will enable him to forge the future. And the fact is that the materialist myth will lose all meaning in a classless society in which there will no longer be either higher or lower.

But, say the Marxists, if you teach man he is free, you betray him since he then no longer needs to become so. Can you imagine a freeborn man demanding his liberation? To which I reply that if man is not originally free, but determined once and for all, you cannot even conceive what his liberation might mean. Some tell me, 'we shall divest human nature of the constraints that deform it.' Such people are fools. What can a man's nature be apart from what he is concretely in his present existence? How could a Marxist believe in a true human nature that would merely be masked by the circumstances of oppression? Others claim they are bringing about human happiness. But what is a happiness that would not be felt and experienced? Happiness is, in its essence, subjectivity. How could it survive under the reign of objectivity?

The only outcome one can really hope to achieve, assuming universal determinism and taking the viewpoint of objectivity, is a more rational organization of society, but what value can such an organization retain if it is not experienced as such by a free subjectivity and transcended in the direction of new ends. There is, in fact, no opposition between these two demands of action—namely, that the agent should be free and the world in which he acts should be determined. For it is not from the same standpoint or in relation to the same realities that one subscribes to the two: freedom is a structure of human action and appears only in commitment [engagement]; determinism is the law of the world. Moreover, action demands only partial linkages and local constants.

In the same way, it is not true that a free man cannot wish to be liberated. For it is not in the same respects that he is free and in chains. His freedom is, as it were, the illumination of the situation into which he is thrown. But the freedom of others may make the situation untenable for him, may drive him to revolt or death. Though the work of slaves manifests their freedom, that work is, nonetheless, imposed, crushing and corrosive; the fruits of their labours are spirited away from them; they are isolated by their work, excluded from a society that exploits them and with which they feel no solidarity, pressed up as they are against matter by a vis a tergo. It is the case that they are merely links in a chain of which they know neither the beginning nor the end; it is true that the master's gaze, his ideology and his commands tend to deny them any existence other than the material. It is precisely by becoming revolutionaries, that is, by organizing the other members of their class to reject the tyranny of their masters, that they will best manifest their freedom. Oppression leaves them no choice but resignation or revolution. But, in each case, they manifest their freedom to choose. And, lastly, whatever goal is assigned to the revolutionary, he goes beyond it and sees it merely as one stage. If he seeks security or a better material organization of society, it is in order that they may serve him as a point of departure.

This was the Marxists' own reply when, in response to some minor wage-claim, reactionaries spoke of the 'sordid materialism of the masses'. They gave it to be understood that behind these material demands there was the assertion of a humanism, that these workers were not just calling for a few shillings more but that their demand was, so to speak, the concrete symbol of their need to be treated as human beings. Human beings, that is to say, freedoms in possession of their own destiny.[22] This remark is valid so far as the revolutionary's ultimate goal is concerned. Beyond the rational organization of the community, class consciousness calls for a new humanism; it is an alienated freedom that has taken freedom as its goal. Socialism is simply the means that will enable the reign of freedom to be achieved; a materialist socialism is, therefore, contradictory, because socialism sets as its goal a humanism that materialism renders inconceivable.

A feature of idealism that particularly disgusts the revolutionary is the tendency to represent changes in

---

22 Marx himself lays this out admirably in his *Economical and Philosophical Manuscripts* (1844).

the world as governed by ideas or, better, as changes in ideas. Death, unemployment, poverty, hunger and the suppression of strikes are not ideas. They are every-day realities that are experienced with abhorrence. They doubtless have a meaning, but they retain, above all, a basic irrational opacity. The 1914 war was not, as Louis Chevalier said, 'Descartes against Kant'; it was the inexpiable deaths of twelve million young men. The revolutionary, crushed beneath reality, refuses to let it be conjured away. He knows the revolution will not be a mere consumption of ideas, but that it will cost blood, sweat and human lives. It is his business to know that things are solid and can, at times, pose insuperable obstacles, that the best-conceived project encounters resistances that some-times make it fail. He knows action is not a happy combination of ideas, but a whole man's effort against the stubborn impenetrability of the universe. He knows that, when the meanings of things have been deciphered, there remains an unassimilable residue—the otherness, irrationality and opaqueness of the real—and that it is this residue that eventually stifles and crushes. Unlike the idealist, whose sloppy thinking he condemns, he sees himself as hard-headed. More than this, against the countervailing power of things he wants to pit not ideas but that action that ulti-mately involves effort, exhausting fatigue and sleepless nights.

Here again, materialism seems to offer him the most satisfying expression of his demand since it asserts the predominance of impenetrable matter over ideas. For materialism, all is fact, conflicts of forces, action. Thought itself becomes a real phenomenon in a measurable world; it is produced by matter and consumes energy. It is in terms of realism that the famous pre- eminence of the object must be conceived. But is this interpretation so deeply satisfying? Does it not overshoot its aim and mystify the demand that gave birth to it? If it is true that nothing seems less like effort than the generation of ideas one by another, effort vanishes just as quickly if we regard the universe as a balance of diverse forces. Nothing gives less of an impression of effort than a force applied to a material point: it does the work of which it is capable, no more and no less, and transforms itself mechanically into kinetic or calorific energy. Nowhere and in no case does nature of itself give us the impression of resistance overcome, of revolt and submission, of weariness. In every circumstance it is everything it can be and that is all. And opposing forces are reconciled, in accordance with the serene laws of mechanics. For reality to be described as a resistance to be overcome by work, that resistance has to be experienced by a subjectivity seeking to conquer it. Nature conceived as pure objectivity is the opposite of the idea. But, precisely on that account, it transforms itself into an idea;

it is the pure idea of objectivity. The real vanishes. For the real is what is impermeable to a subjectivity: it is this lump of sugar which, as Bergson says, I must wait to see melt, or, if you prefer, it is the subject's obligation to experience such a wait. It is the human project; it is my thirst which determines that it 'takes a long time' to melt. Outside of human concerns, it melts neither slowly nor quickly but precisely in a time that depends on its nature, its density and the quantity of water in which it is soaking.

It is human subjectivity that discovers the adversity of the real in and through the project it forms of transcending it in the direction of the future. For a hill to be easy or hard to climb, someone has to have formed the project of ascending it. Idealism and materialism both make the real disappear, the one because it eliminates the thing, the other because it eliminates subjectivity. For reality to reveal itself, a human being has to struggle against it. In a word, the revolutionary's realism requires the existence both of the world and of subjectivity. More than this, it requires such a correlation between the two that one cannot conceive a subjectivity apart from the world or a world that would not be illuminated by the effort of a subjectivity.[23] The maximum reality, the maximum resistance will

---

23 This is, once again, Marx's view in 1844, that is to say, before the ill-starred meeting with Engels.

be obtained if we assume that human beings are by definition in-situation-in-the-world and that they learn the difficult lesson of reality by defining themselves in relation to it.

Let us note here, in fact, that too close an adherence to universal determinism runs the risk of eliminating any resistance on the part of reality. This was proved to me in a conversation with M. Garaudy and two of his comrades. I asked them if matters really were cut and dried when Stalin signed the Russo-German Pact and when the French Communists decided to participate in de Gaulle's government; I wondered whether those responsible had not run risks with these decisions, feeling rather anxious about their responsibilities. For it seems to me that the chief characteristic of reality is that we are never on totally firm ground with it and the consequences of our acts are merely probable. But M. Garaudy interrupted me: for him, matters are cut and dried in advance; there is a science of history and the facts follow in a strict sequence. One is therefore making a safe bet. He was so carried away by his zeal that he ended up saying excitedly, 'And what does Stalin's intelligence matter? I don't give a fig for it!' It must be added that, under the stern glances of his comrades, he blushed, lowered his eyes and added with quite a pious air, 'though Stalin is very intelligent.'

Unlike revolutionary realism, then, which states that the least little result is achieved only with difficulty, amid the greatest uncertainty, the materialist myth leads some to be profoundly reassured about the outcome of their efforts. As they see it, they cannot but succeed. History is a science, its findings are written down, one has only to read them. This attitude is quite patently escapist. The revolutionary has overturned the bourgeois myths and the working class has undertaken, through a thousand vicissitudes, through snubs and climb-downs, victories and defeats, to forge its own destiny in freedom and in anguish. But our Garaudys are afraid. What they look for in Communism is not liberation, but a heightened discipline. They fear nothing so much as freedom. And if they have thrown off the a priori values of the class from which they came, they have done so only to recover a prioris of knowledge and paths already marked out in history. There are no risks, no worries. All is safe, the outcomes are assured. As a result, reality vanishes and history is reduced to an idea unfolding itself.

Inside this idea, M. Garaudy feels safe. Communist intellectuals to whom I reported this conversation shrugged their shoulders; 'Garaudy is a scientist,' they informed me contemptuously. 'He is a Protestant bourgeois who, for his own edification, has replaced the finger of God with historical materialism.' I am quite willing to accept this and I will admit too that

M. Garaudy didn't seem to me to be a shining light. But he writes a lot and the Communists do not disown him. And it is no accident that most scientists have found a home in the Communist Party and that that party, so severe on heresy, does not condemn them.

We must repeat the point here: if revolutionaries wish to act, they cannot regard historical events as the outcome of arbitrary contingencies. But they do not in any sense demand that the road be preordained for them. On the contrary, they wish to find it for themselves. Some constants, certain partial series and structural laws within determinate social forms are what they need to do their planning. If you give them more, everything vanishes into ideas: history no longer has to be made, but can merely be read off day by day; the real becomes a dream.

We were enjoined to choose between materialism and idealism, and we were told we would be able to find no middle way between the two doctrines. We have allowed the exigencies of revolution to speak without preconceived ideas and we have found that these themselves marked out the lineaments of an original philosophy that rejects both idealism and materialism. It emerged for us, first, that the revolutionary act was the free act par excellence. Not with an anarchistic, individualist freedom; if that were the case, then the revolutionary, by his very situation, could only demand, more or less explicitly, the rights of the 'exquisite class', or, in other words, his integration into the upper social strata. But since he calls from within the oppressed class—and for the whole of it—for a more rational social status, his freedom lies in the act by which he demands the liberation of all his class and, more generally, of all human beings. It is, at its source, a recognition of other freedoms, and it demands to be recognized by them. Thus it places itself, from the outset, on the footing of solidarity. And the revolutionary act contains within itself the premises of a philosophy of freedom or, rather, by its very existence, creates that philosophy. But as, at the same time, the revolutionary discovers himself by and in his free project, as an oppressed person within an oppressed class, his original position requires that his oppression be explained to him. This means once again that human beings are free—for there can be no oppression of matter by matter, merely a balance of forces—and that a certain relationship may exist between freedoms, such that the one does not recognize the other and acts from outside it to transform it into an object. And reciprocally, since oppressed freedom seeks to liberate itself by force, the revolutionary attitude demands a theory of violence as a riposte to oppression. Here too, materialist terms are as inadequate for explaining violence as the conceptions of idealism.

Idealism, which is a philosophy of digestion and assimilation, does not even conceive the absolute, insurmountable pluralism of freedoms pitted one against another: idealism is a monism. But materialism is also a monism: there is no 'battle of opposites' within material unity. To tell the truth, there aren't even any opposites: hot and cold are merely different degrees on the thermometric scale; we pass progressively from light to darkness. Two equal and opposing forces cancel each other out and produce merely a state of equilibrium. The idea of a battle of opposites is the projection of human relationships on to material ones.

A revolutionary philosophy must account for the plurality of freedoms and show how each, while being a freedom for itself, must at the same time be able to be an object for others. Only this twofold character of freedom and objectivity can explain the complex notions of oppression, struggle, failure and violence. For it is only ever a freedom that is oppressed, but it can be oppressed only if it lends itself in some way to oppression; that is to say, if it presents the outward appearance of a thing to the Other. The revolutionary movement and its project, which is to take society by violence from a state in which freedoms are alienated to another state based on the mutual recognition of those freedoms, is to be understood in these terms.

Similarly, the revolutionary who experiences oppression bodily and in every one of his actions, in no way wishes to either underestimate the yoke under which he labours or tolerate idealist criticism dissipating that yoke into ideas. At the same time, he contests the rights of the privileged class and thereby destroys the idea of rights in general. But it would be a mistake to believe, as the materialist does, that he does so in order to replace them by facts, plain and simple. For facts can generate only facts, not representations of facts; the present generates another present, not the future. So the revolutionary act requires that the opposition between materialism—which can account for the disintegration of a society, but not the construction of a new one—and idealism—which confers a de jure existence on facts—be transcended in the unity of a synthesis. It calls for a new philosophy that takes a different view of human relations with the world.

If revolution is to be possible, human beings must be as contingent as facts; and yet they must differ from facts by their practical power to prepare the future and, consequently, to go beyond the present, to rise above their situation. This 'rising-above' is not in any sense comparable to the negative movement by which the Stoic attempts to take refuge within himself; it is by projecting themselves forward, by committing themselves to undertakings, that revolutionaries transcend the present. And since they are human beings acting like human beings, we must attribute to all human activity this ability to 'rise above'. The slightest human gesture is to be understood in terms of the future; even the reactionary is oriented towards the future, since his concern is to prepare a future identical to the past.

The absolute realism of the tactician demands that human beings be immersed in the real, threatened by concrete dangers, victims of concrete oppression from which they will free themselves by equally concrete action. Blood, sweat, pain and death are not ideas; the rock that crushes, the bullet that kills are not ideas. But for things to reveal what Bachelard rightly calls their 'coefficient of adversity', it takes the light of a project that illuminates them, be it merely the very simple and rudimentary one of living. It is untrue, then, as the idealist contends, that man is outside the world and nature, or that, like a reluctant bather, he has only dipped into it, keeping his head in a nobler air. He is entirely in the clutches of nature, which can crush him at any moment and destroy him body and soul. He is in nature's clutches from the very beginning: to be born really does mean 'coming into the world' in a situation not of his own choosing, with this body, this family and perhaps also this race. But if he does, indeed, plan to 'change the world', as Marx expressly states, that means he is originally a being for whom the world exists in its totality; this is something a lump of phosphorus or lead will never be, being merely a part of the world, played upon by forces to which it uncomprehendingly submits. This is because he transcends the world in the direction of a future state from which he can contemplate it, for it is by changing the world that we are able to know it. Neither the detached consciousness that would soar above the universe without being able to achieve a standpoint on it, nor the material object, which reflects a state of the world without comprehending it, can ever 'grasp' the totality of the existent in a synthesis—even a purely conceptual one. Only a human being in situation in the universe can do this, entirely weighed down as he is by the forces of nature, but transcending those forces totally by his project of harnessing them.

It is these new notions of 'situation' and 'being-in-the-world' which the revolutionary demands concretely, by the whole of his behaviour, to have elucidated. And if he escapes from the thickets of rights and duties into which the idealist attempts to mislead him, it should not be simply to fall into defiles narrowly marked out for him by the materialist. No doubt intelligent Marxists do acknowledge a certain contingency in history, but only to say that, if socialism fails, humanity will sink into barbarism. In short, if the constructive forces are to win out, historical determinism assigns them only one path. But there may be many kinds of barbarism and many socialisms—and perhaps even a barbaric socialism. What the revolutionary calls for is the possibility of human beings inventing their own law. This is the basis of his humanism and his socialism. Deep down, he does not think—at least in his unmystified moments—that socialism is waiting for him just around history's corner, like a robber with a cudgel in some corner of the woods. He believes socialism is something he is making and, having shaken off all rights and dashed them to the ground, he grants socialism no other entitlement to existence than the fact that the revolutionary class invents it, wants it and will build it. Hence, the slow, ruthless conquest of socialism is nothing other than the affirmation, in and through history, of human freedom. And precisely because man is free, the triumph of socialism is not certain at all. It does not stand at the end of the road, like some milestone, but is the human project. It will be what human beings make it; this is what emerges from the gravity with which the revolutionary contemplates his action. He not only feels responsible for the coming of a socialist republic in general, but for the particular nature of that socialism.

Thus revolutionary philosophy, transcending both the idealist thinking that is bourgeois and the materialist myth that suited the oppressed masses for a time, aspires to be the philosophy of humanity in general. And it is quite natural that it should: if it is to be true, it will, in fact, be universal. The ambiguity of materialism is that it claims at times to be a class ideology and, at others, to be the expression of absolute truth. But the revolutionary, in his very choice of revolution, takes a privileged position: he does not fight for the preservation of a class, like the activist in the bourgeois parties, but for the elimination of classes; he does not divide society into men by divine right and natural men or Untermenschen, but calls for the unification of ethnic groups and classes—in a word, for the unity of all human beings; he does not allow himself to be mystified by rights and duties lodged a priori in an intelligible heaven, but posits, in the very act of revolt against them, human freedom, metaphysical and entire; he is the human being who wishes human beings to assume their destiny freely and totally. So his cause is essentially the cause of humanity and his philosophy must speak the truth about humanity.

But, you will say, if it is universal, that is to say, true for all, is it not by that same token beyond parties and classes? Are we not back with apolitical, asocial, rootless idealism? My answer is that this philosophy can reveal itself, at first, only to revolutionaries or, in other words, to people who are in the situation of oppressed persons, and that it needs them to manifest itself in the world. But it is true that it must be able to be the philosophy of every human being, insofar as a bourgeois oppressor is himself oppressed by his own oppression. For, to keep the oppressed classes under his rule, he must pay with his own person and become enmeshed in the tangle of rights and duties he has invented.

If the revolutionary retains the materialist myth, the young bourgeois can come to the revolution only through the perception of social injustices; he comes to it out of individual generosity, which is always suspect, since the source of generosity may dry up, and he faces the additional ordeal of swallowing a materialism that is inimical to his reason and that does not express his personal situation. But if the revolutionary philosophy is once made explicit, the bourgeois who has criticized the ideology of his class, who has recognized his contingency and freedom, who has understood that that freedom can be asserted only through the recognition bestowed on it by other freedoms, will discover that this philosophy speaks to him of himself, insofar as he wishes to strip away the mystifying apparatus of the bourgeois class and assert himself as a human being among others. At that point, revolutionary humanism will not appear to him as the philosophy of an oppressed class but as the Truth itself—the truth humiliated, masked, oppressed by human beings whose interests lie in flight from it. And it will become manifest to all persons of goodwill that it is truth that is revolutionary. Not the abstract Truth of idealism, but the concrete truth—the truth willed, created, maintained and won through social struggle by human beings working for the liberation of humanity.

It will perhaps be objected that this analysis of revolutionary demands is abstract, since ultimately the only existing revolutionaries are Marxists and they subscribe to materialism. It is true that the Communist Party is the only revolutionary party. And it is true that materialism is the Party's doctrine. But I have not been attempting to describe what Marxists believe, but to tease out the implications of what it is that they do. And frequenting Communists has taught me that nothing is more variable, abstract and subjective than what is termed their Marxism. What could be more different from M. Garaudy's naive, stubborn scientism than M. Hervé's philosophy? You may say that difference reflects the difference in their intelligences and this is true. But, above all, it indicates the degree of awareness each has of his deep attitude and the degree to which each believes in the materialist myth. It is not by accident that there is said to be a crisis in Marxist thinking today and that Marxism is resigned to having people like Garaudy as its spokesmen. The Communists are caught between the obsolescence of the materialist myth and the fear of introducing division, or at least hesitation, into their ranks by adopting a new ideology.

The best have fallen silent; the silence has been filled up with the chatter of imbeciles. 'After all,' the leaders no doubt think, 'what does ideology matter? Our old ideology has proved its worth and will no doubt lead us to victory. Our struggle isn't about ideas: it is a political and social struggle between human beings.' No doubt they are right so far as the present and the near future are concerned. But what kind of human beings will they make? You cannot get away with training generations of human beings by teaching them errors that happen to work. What will happen if one day materialism suffocates the revolutionary project?

Les Temps modernes (June 1946)

✳

THE ARTIST AND HIS CONSCIENCE

You have asked me, my dear Leibowitz, to append a few words to your book. The fact is that I happened to write some time ago on the subject of literary commitment and, by linking our names together, you wish to indicate that artists and writers stand shoulder to shoulder in their common concerns in any one period. If friendship had not been sufficient, the concern to show this solidarity would have made up my mind for me. But now I have to put pen to paper, I confess I feel very awkward.

I have no particular competence in music and I don't want to invite ridicule by repeating badly and in inappropriate terms what you have put so well in the appropriate language. Nor would I foolishly presume to introduce you to readers who already know you extremely well and who follow you passionately in your threefold career as composer, conductor and music critic. It would be a pleasure to say how good I think your book is—it is so simple and clear, it taught me so much, it clears up the most confused and intricate problems, teaching us to take a new perspective on them—but what purpose would that serve? The reader doesn't need me for that: to appreciate its virtues, he simply has to open the book. In the end, the best I can do is to assume we are chatting, as we have done so often, and unburden myself of the concerns and questions your work raised for me. You have convinced me, yet I feel uneasy and have misgivings. I must tell you about them. In so doing, I am, of course, a layman questioning an initiate, a pupil talking over the lesson with the teacher. But, after all, many of your readers are lay people and I imagine my feelings reflect theirs. All in all, this preface has no other aim than to ask you, in their name and mine, to write a new book, or just an article, in which you would remove our last remaining doubts.

The queasy condition of the Communist boa, incapable either of keeping down or coughing up the enormous Picasso, gives me no cause for amusement. In the Communist Party's indigestion, I discern the symptoms of an infection that extends to the whole of our age.

When the privileged classes are happily ensconced in their principles, when they have good consciences, when the oppressed, duly convinced that they are inferior creatures, pride themselves on their servile condition, the artist is at ease. Since the Renaissance, the musician has, you say, constantly addressed himself to an audience of specialists. Yet what was this audience but the ruling aristocracy, which, not content with exerting military, judicial, political and administrative power over the whole land, at some point also appointed itself the arbiter of taste? Since this divine-right elite decided what was or was not human, the cantor or *Kapellmeister* could direct their symphonies or cantatas to the whole of humanity. Art could call itself humanistic because society remained inhuman.

Is it the same today? This is the question which torments me and which, in turn, I put to you. For the ruling classes of our Western societies can no longer dream of claiming that they are, themselves, the measure of humanity. The oppressed classes are conscious of their strength; they possess their own rites, techniques and ideology. Of the proletariat Rosenberg says, admirably:

> On the one hand, the present social order is permanently threatened by the extraordinary potential power of the workers; on the other, the fact that this power is in the hands of an

anonymous category, a historical 'zero', gives all modern mythmakers the temptation to treat the working class as the raw material for new collectivities, through which society can be subjugated. Cannot this history-less proletariat be so easily converted into *anything*, as into itself? Holding in suspense the drama between revolution by the working class on its own account and revolution as an instrument for others, the pathos of the proletariat dominates modern history.[1]

Now music, to speak only of this one art, has indeed undergone a metamorphosis. The art of music took its laws and limits from what it believed to be its essence; you have shown brilliantly how, at the end of a rigorous and yet free development, music wrested itself from alienation and set about creating its essence for itself by freely providing its own laws. Could it not, then, for its humble part, influence the course of history by helping to present the working classes with the image of a 'total man' who, having wrested himself from alienation and from the myth of human 'nature', forges in daily battle his essence and the values by which he judges himself?

---

1 See Harold Rosenberg, 'Le Prolétariat comme héros et comme rôle', *Les Temps modernes*, 56 (June 1950): 2151.

When it recognizes *a priori* limitations, music, in spite of itself, reinforces alienation, celebrates *the given* and, while manifesting freedom in its own way, indicates that that freedom is bounded by nature. It is not uncommon for the 'mythmakers' to employ music to mystify audiences by communicating a sacred emotion to them, as is the case, for example, with military bands or choirs. But if I understand you aright, should we not see in the more recent forms of this art something like the presentation of the raw power of creation? And I believe I grasp here what sets you against those Communist musicians who signed the *Prague Manifesto*: they would like the artist to subject himself to an object-society and to sing the praises of the Soviet world as Haydn sang the praises of the divine Creation.[2] They call on him to copy what *is*, to imitate without transcending and to offer his audience the example of submission to an established order; if music defined itself as a permanent revolution, would it not risk, for its part, awakening in its listeners the desire to transport that revolution into other fields? You, by contrast, wish to show man that he is not prefabricated, that he never will be, and that he always

---

2 On 20–29 May 1948, the Second International Congress of Composers was held in Prague. The conclusions of the congress, where it had been argued that contemporary Western music was in a state of crisis, were formulated in one of the official Congress documents, entitled the Proclamation (*Provolani*) but also known as the *Prague Manifesto*. [Trans.]

and everywhere retains the freedom to act and to *make himself*, above and beyond any kind of 'prefabrication'.

But here's what troubles me: haven't you established that an inner dialectic took music from monody to polyphony and from the simplest polyphonic forms to the most complex? This means that it can go forward, but not back: it would be as naive to wish to return it to its earlier forms as to wish to reduce our industrial societies to pastoral simplicity. This is all well and good, but, as a result, music's increasing complexity reserves it—as you recognize yourself—for a handful of specialists who are necessarily recruited from within the privileged class. Schönberg is further removed from the workers than Mozart was, in his day, from the peasants. You will tell me that most bourgeois have no understanding of music, and that would be true. But it is also true that those who can appreciate it belong to the bourgeoisie, enjoy the advantages of bourgeois culture and are generally members of the professions. I know that its *amateurs* are not rich; they are to be found mainly among the middle classes; it is rare for a big industrialist to be a music-lover. However, that does happen, whereas I don't remember seeing a worker at your concerts.

It is certain, then, that modern music breaks with established patterns, spurns convention and marks out its own path. But to whom does it speak of liberation, freedom, will and the creation of man by man? To a stale, genteel audience, whose ears are clotted with an idealist aesthetic. It says, 'permanent revolution' and the bourgeoisie hears 'Evolution and Progress'. And even if some among the young intellectuals understand it, won't their present impotence lead them to see this liberation as a fine myth but not as *their* reality?

Let us be clear about this: it is the fault neither of the artist nor the art. Art has not changed *from within*: its movement, negativity and creative force remain what they always were. Today, as yesterday, what Malraux wrote remains true: 'All creation is, initially, the struggle of a potential form against an imitated one.'[3] And it has to be that way. But in the heavens above our modern societies, the appearance of those enormous planets, the masses, overturns everything, transforms artistic activity from a distance, without even touching it, strips it of its meaning and undermines the artist's good conscience: simply because the masses are *also* struggling for man, but blindly, because they run the constant risk of going astray, of forgetting what they are, of allowing themselves to be seduced by the voice of a mythmaker, and because the artist does not have the language that would enable them to hear him. It is indeed of *their* freedom that he speaks—for there is only one freedom—but he speaks of it in a foreign language.

3 André Malraux, *The Voices of Silence: Man and His Art* (Princeton, NJ: Princeton University Press, 1978).

The disarray in which the cultural policy of the USSR finds itself would be sufficient to prove that what is involved here is a historical contradiction essential to our age, not some bourgeois outrage due to the subjectivism of artists. Of course, if one takes the view that the USSR is the Devil, one may suppose that its leaders take an evil delight in carrying out purges that bewilder artists and exhaust them. And if one thinks that God is Soviet, there is no difficulty either: God acts justly and that is all there is to it. But if we dare for a moment to argue the new, paradoxical thesis that the Soviet leaders are human beings—human beings in a difficult, virtually untenable position, who are trying to do what seems right to them, who are often overtaken by events and who are sometimes carried further than they would like; in short, human beings like us—then everything changes, and we may suppose that they take no pleasure in making these sudden changes of tack that are in danger of throwing the whole machine out of kilter. In destroying classes, the Russian Revolution proposed to destroy elites, that is, those exquisite, parasitic organs one finds in all societies of oppression—organs that produce values and works like papal bulls. Wherever an elite functions—the aristocracy of the aristocracy limning out for aristocrats the figure of the total man—then, instead of enriching the oppressed, the new values and the works of art increase their impoverishment in absolute terms: for the majority of human beings, the products of the elite are rejections, absences and limits. The taste of our 'art-lovers' necessarily defines the bad taste or tastelessness of the working classes, and, when a work is fêted by refined minds, there is in the world one more 'treasure' that the workers will not possess, one more thing of beauty they can neither appreciate nor understand. Values can be a positive determination for each only if they are the common product of all. A new acquisition on the part of society, be it a new industrial technique or a new form of expression, being made by everyone, must, for each person, be an enrichment of the world and a path opening up—in short, it must represent that society's innermost potential. Instead of the total man of the aristocracy defining himself by the totality of the opportunities he denies to everyone, as the person who knows what others do not, who appreciates what they cannot appreciate, who does what they do not do—in short, as the most irreplaceable of human beings—the total man of the socialist societies would be defined at birth by the totality of opportunities that all offer to each and at his death by the new opportunities—however small they may be—that he has offered to all. In this way, *all* are the path of each to himself and each is the path of all to all.

But at the same time as it sought to bring a socialist aesthetic into being, the needs of administration, industrialization and war prompted the USSR to implement first a policy of training *cadres*: it needed engineers, functionaries and military leaders. Hence the danger that this *de facto* elite, whose culture, occupations and standard of living were in marked contrast to those of the masses, would in turn produce values and myths; the danger that 'art-lovers' would arise within it who would create a *special* demand for artists. The Chinese text that you quote, revised by Jean Paulhan, sums up quite appositely the threat that hovers over a society under construction: if horse-lovers are enough to bring fine steeds into being, then an elite that formed itself into a specialist audience would be enough to bring into being an art for the elite. There is a danger that a new segregation may occur: a culture of cadres will be born, with its accompaniment of abstract values and esoteric works, whereas the mass of the workers will fall back into a new barbarism that can be gauged precisely by their failure to understand the products aimed at that new elite. This, I believe, is one of the explanations for those infamous purges that revolt us: as the cadres strengthen their position, as the bureaucracy is in danger of transforming itself if not into a class then at least into an oppressive elite, a tendency towards aestheticism develops in the artist. And, while drawing on support from this elite, the leaders have to strive to maintain, at least ideally, the principle of a community producing its values as a whole. They are most surely forced into contradictory projects, since they are conducting a general policy of producing cadres and a mass-based cultural policy: with one hand they are creating an elite, while with the other they are attempting to wrest its ideology from it, though this is constantly re-emerging and always will. But, conversely, there is indeed confusion among the opponents of the USSR when they criticize its leaders for simultaneously creating both an oppressor class and yet wishing to smash class aesthetics. What is true is that the Soviet leaders and the artists of the bourgeois societies are faced with the same impasse: music has developed according to its own dialectic; it has become an art based on a complex technique; it is a regrettable fact, but *a fact nonetheless*, that it needs a specialized audience. In short, modern music requires an elite and the working masses require music. How is this conflict to be resolved? By 'giving form to the deep popular sensibility'? But *what* form? Vincent d'Indy made serious music 'on a French mountain air'. Do we believe the mountain-dwellers would have recognized their song? And then the popular sensibility creates its own forms. Folk songs, jazz, African chants have no need of being reworked by professional artists. On the contrary, the application of a complex technique to the spontaneous products of that sensibility would necessarily distort them. This is the tragedy of the Haitian artists who cannot manage to connect their formal culture to the folk subjects they would like to treat. The *Prague Manifesto* says, more or less, that we have to lower the level of music while at the same time raising the cultural level of the masses. Either this means nothing or it is an admission that art and its public can unite only in absolute mediocrity. You are right to point out that the conflict between art and society is eternal because it relates to the essence of each. But, in our day, it has assumed a new, more acute form: art is a permanent revolution and, for forty years, the fundamental situation of our societies has been revolutionary. Now, social revolution demands an aesthetic conservatism, whereas the aesthetic revolution, in spite of the artist himself, demands a social conservatism. Picasso, a sincere Communist condemned by the Soviet leaders, and purveyor of works of art to rich American art-lovers, is the living image of this contradiction. As for Fougeron, his paintings have stopped pleasing the elite but never stirred up any interest among the proletariat.

Moreover, the contradiction becomes deeper and sharper when we come to the sources of musical inspiration. It is a question, says the *Prague Manifesto*, of expressing 'the sentiments and the lofty progressive ideas of the popular masses'. I can agree on the sentiments, but how on earth are 'the lofty progressive ideas' to be turned into music? For music is, in the end, a *non-signifying* art. Unrigorous minds have happily spoken of a 'musical language'. But we know very well that the 'musical phrase' does not refer to any object: it is itself an object. How could this dumb thing evoke man's destiny for him? The *Prague Manifesto* offers a solution of entertaining naivety: 'the musical forms that enable us to achieve these goals' will be cultivated: 'in particular, vocal music, opera, oratorio, cantatas and choral works, etc.' Why, of course: these hybrid works have the gift of the gab; they are musical chatterers. There could be no better way to say that music is to be merely a pretext, a means of enhancing the glory of the word. It is words that will hymn Stalin, the Five Year Plan and the electrification of the Soviet Union. With other words, the same music might celebrate Pétain, Churchill, Truman or the Tennessee Valley Authority. Change the lyrics and a hymn to the Russian dead of Stalingrad will become a funeral oration for the Germans who fell before that same city. What can sounds provide? A great blast of sonorous heroism; it is the word that will bring specificity. There could be musical commitment [*engagement*] only if the work were such that it were susceptible to only one verbal commentary; in short, the sound structure would have to *repel* some words and *attract* others. Is this possible? In some privileged cases, perhaps: and you yourself quote

A Survivor from Warsaw.[4] And yet Schönberg has not been able to avoid recourse to words. How, without the words, would we recognize in this 'gallop of wild horses' the counting of the dead? We would hear a gallop. The poetic comparison is not in the music, but in the relation of the music to the words. But, you will say, here at least the words are part of the work; they are of themselves a musical element. That is so, but must we give up the sonata, the quartet, the symphony? Must we devote ourselves to 'operas, oratorios and cantatas', as the *Prague Manifesto* urges? I know you do not think so. And I agree with you when you write that, 'the subject chosen remains a *neutral* element, something like a raw material that will have to be subjected to a purely artistic treatment. It is only in the last analysis that the quality of this treatment will prove or disprove that . . . extra-artistic concerns and emotions belong to the purely artistic project.'

Only, in that case, I can no longer very clearly see where musical commitment lies. I fear it may have fled the work to take refuge in the artist's conduct, in his

---

4 *A Survivor from Warsaw, Op. 46 (Ein Überlebender aus Warschau)* is a work for narrator, men's chorus, and orchestra written by the Austrian composer Arnold Schönberg in 1947. The initial inspiration was a suggestion from the Russian émigrée dancer Corinne Chochem for a work to pay tribute to the Jewish victims of the German Third Reich. [Trans.]

attitude to art. The life of the musician may be exemplary—his voluntary poverty, his rejection of easy success, his constant dissatisfaction and the permanent revolution he pursues against others and himself—but I fear the austere morality of his person may remain a commentary external to his work. The musical work is not *by itself* negativity, rejection of traditions and liberatory movement; it is the positive consequence of this rejection and negativity. As a sound object, it no more reveals the doubts, crises of despair or final decision of the composer than the inventor's patent reveals the torments and worries of the inventor. It does not show us the dissolution of the old rules: it shows us *other rules*, which are the positive laws of its development. Now, the artist must not be the commentary on his work for the public: if the music is committed music, then it is in the sound object as it presents itself immediately to the ear, without reference to the artist or to earlier traditions, that the commitment, in its intuitive reality, will be found.

Is this possible? It seems we run up here, in another form, against the dilemma we encountered initially: by enlisting music, a non-signifying art, to express pre-established significations, one alienates it; but by rejecting the significations into what you call 'the extra-artistic', doesn't musical liberation run the risk of leading to abstraction and presenting the composer as an example of that formal, purely negative freedom Hegel calls Terror? Servitude or Terror: it is possible that our age offers no other alternative to the artist.[5] If I have to choose, I confess that I prefer Terror: not for itself but because, in these lean years, it maintains the properly aesthetic demands of art and enables it to await more propitious times without suffering too much damage.

But I must confess that, before I read your book, I was less pessimistic. I present here my very naive sense as a relatively uncultured listener: when someone performed a musical composition in front of me, I found no signification of any kind in the succession of sounds, and it was of no matter to me whatever whether Beethoven had composed one of his funeral marches 'for the death of a hero' or whether, at the end of his first Ballade, Chopin had wanted to suggest the satanic laughter of Wallenrod; on the other hand, it did seem to me that that succession had a *meaning*, and it is that meaning I liked. I have, in fact, always distinguished meaning from signification. It seems to me that an object signifies when one aims, through it, at another object. In this case, the mind does not attend to the sign itself, but passes beyond it to the thing signified; it frequently happens, even, that this

---

5 Let me make clear that the artist, in my view, differs from the writer [*littérateur*] in that he cultivates non-signifying arts. I have shown elsewhere that the problems of literature are very different.

thing remains present to us when we have long forgotten the words that made us conceive it. Meaning, on the other hand, is not distinct from the thing itself, and the more we attend to the thing it inhabits, the more manifest it is. I shall say that an object has a *meaning* when it is the incarnation of a reality that transcends it but which one cannot grasp outside of it and which its infinite nature makes impossible to express adequately by any system of signs; it is always a totality that is involved: the totality of a person, of a milieu, of an age or of the human condition. Of the *Mona Lisa*'s smile I shall say that it does not 'mean' *to say* anything, but that it has a meaning: through it is realized the strange mixture of mysticism and naturalism, of self-evidence and mystery that characterizes the Renaissance. And I need only look at it to distinguish it from that other, equally mysterious, but more troubling, stiffer, ironic, naive and sacred smile that floats vaguely on the lips of the Etruscan Apollo or the 'hideous', secular, rationalistic, witty smile shown in Houdon's *Voltaire*. Of course, Voltaire's smile had a *significance*; it appeared on particular occasions and *intended to say*, 'I'm not fooled' or, 'Listen to this fanatic!' But, at the same time, it is Voltaire himself, Voltaire as ineffable totality: of Voltaire you can speak *ad infinitum*; his existential reality cannot be encompassed in words. But as soon as he smiles, there you *have* the whole of him, effortlessly. Now, it seemed to me that music was a pretty, dumb creature with deeply meaningful eyes. When I hear a Brandenburg Concerto, I never *think* of the eighteenth century, of the austerity of Leipzig, the Puritan ponderousness of the German princes, of that moment in the history of the mind when reason, in full possession of its techniques, remained nonetheless subordinate to faith and when the logic of the concept transformed itself into a logic of judgement. And yet it is all there, given in the sounds, in the same way as the Renaissance smiles on the lips of *La Gioconda*. And I have always thought that the 'average' listener who, like me, has no particular precise knowledge about the history of musical composition, could immediately date a work by Scarlatti, Schumann or Ravel—even if he might get the composer's name wrong—on account of that silent presence in any sound-object of the entire age and its *Weltanschauung*. Is it not conceivable that commitment in music resides at this level? I know what you are going to say to me: if the artist has painted himself wholly in his work—and his century with him—then he did so involuntarily: his only concern was to make music. And it is audiences today who, a hundred years later, discern intentions that are in the object without having been put there: the listener of the last century perceived only the melody; he saw absolute and *natural* rules in what we retrospectively regard as postulates that reflect the age. This is true: but can we not conceive today of a more self-aware artist who, by thinking about his art, might attempt to embody his human condition in it? I merely ask the question; it is you who are qualified to answer it. But, I confess that if, with you, I condemn the absurd *Prague Manifesto*, I cannot help being disturbed by certain passages in the famous speech by Zhdanov that inspired the whole cultural policy of the USSR.[6] You know as well as I do that the Communists are guilty because they are wrong in their way of being right, and they make us guilty because they are right in their way of being wrong. The *Prague Manifesto* is the extreme, stupid consequence of an entirely defensible theory of art and one that does not necessarily entail aesthetic authoritarianism. We must, said Zhdanov, 'know life, so as to be able to depict it truthfully in works of art, not . . . depict it in a dead, scholastic way, not simply as "objective reality", but . . . depict reality in its revolutionary development.' What did he mean other than that reality is never inert?—it is always changing and those who appreciate it or depict it are themselves changing. The deep unity of all these unavoidable changes is the

6 Speech of 17 August 1934 to the First Soviet Writers' Congress. [Published as 'Soviet Literature—The Richest in Ideas, The Most Advanced Literature', in H. G. Scott (ed. and trans.), *Problems of Soviet Literature: Reports and Speeches at the First Soviet Writers' Congress* (Westport, CT: Hyperion Press, Inc., 1935), pp. 15–24. Also available at: https://bit.ly/-3sr5pSS— Trans.]

future meaning of the whole system. So, the artist must smash those habits that have already crystallized and that make us see *in the present* those institutions and customs that are *already outdated*. To provide a truthful image of our age, he must view it from the heights of the future it is fashioning for itself, since it is tomorrow that decides the truth of today. In a sense, this conception connects with your own: have you not shown that the committed artist is 'ahead of' his time and that he is watching the present traditions of his art with future eyes? There is, most certainly, an allusion in your writing, as in Zhdanov's, to negativity and 'overcoming', but he does not confine himself to the moment of negation. For him, the work's value derives from a positive content: it is a lump of the future that has fallen into the present; it is some years ahead of the judgement we shall pass on ourselves; it opens up our future possibilities; at one and the same time, it follows, accompanies and precedes the dialectical progression of history.

I have always thought there was nothing sillier than those theories that attempt to determine the mental level of a person or a social group. There are no *levels*: for a child to be 'his age' is to be simultaneously above that age and below it. It is the same with our intellectual and sensory habits. Matisse has written, 'Our senses have a developmental age that derives not from the immediate ambience, but from a

moment of civilization.'[7] This is right. And, conversely, they transcend that moment and obscurely
perceive a host of objects that we shall see tomorrow;
they discern another world in this one. But this is not
the product of some prophetic gift: it is the contradictions and conflicts of the age that over-excite the
senses to the point of giving them a kind of double
vision. It is true, then, that a work of art is both an
individual production and a social fact. What we
rediscover in *The Well-tempered Clavier*[8] is not just the
religious, monarchical order: to those prelates and
barons, victims and beneficiaries of oppressive traditions, Bach offered the image of a freedom which,
while appearing to contain itself within traditional
frames, passed beyond tradition in the direction of
new creations. He countered the closed tradition of
the little despotic courts with an open tradition; he
taught how to find originality by consenting to a dis-

---

7 Henri Matisse, 'Statements to Tériade: On the Purity of Means'
[1936], in Jack D. Flam (ed.), *Matisse on Art* (California: University
of California Press, 1995), p. 123 (translation modified). [Trans.]

8 *The Well-tempered Clavier* (*Das Wohltemperirte Clavier*) is a collec-
tion of solo keyboard music composed by Johann Sebastian Bach.
He first gave the title to a book of preludes and fugues in all 24 major
and minor keys, dated 1722, composed 'for the profit and use of
musical youth desirous of learning, and especially for the pastime of
those already skilled in this study'. He later compiled a second book
of the same kind, dated 1742, but titled 'Twenty-four Preludes and
Fugues'. The two works are now usually considered to comprise *The
Well-tempered Clavier* and are referred to respectively as Books I and
II. [Trans.]

cipline—in a word, how to live: he showed the play
of moral liberty within religious and monarchical
absolutism, he depicted the proud dignity of the subject who obeys his king, of the believer who prays to
his God. While being fully in his age, all of whose
prejudices he accepts and reflects, he is at the same
time outside it and judges it wordlessly in terms of the
still implicit rules of a pietistic moralism that will give
rise, half a century later, to the ethics of Kant. And
the infinite variations he executes, the postulates he
forces himself to respect, bring his successors to the
brink of changing the postulates themselves. Admittedly, his life was an example of conformism and I do
not suppose he ever aired any very revolutionary
views. But is his art not simultaneously the magnifi-
cation of obedience and the transcendence of that
obedience, which he *judges*, in the very moment that
he seeks to *show* it to us, from the standpoint of an
individualist rationalism as yet unborn? Later, with no
loss of his aristocratic audience, the artist gains
another one: through his thinking on the recipes of
his art and the continual adjustments he makes to
received custom, he reflects to the bourgeoisie, ahead
of time, the calm, non-revolutionary progression it
wishes to accomplish. Your conception of musical
commitment, my dear Leibowitz, seems to me to suit
that happy age: the match between the aesthetic
demands on the artist and the political demands on

his listeners is so perfect that a single critical analysis serves to demonstrate the wicked futility of internal customs barriers, tolls and feudal rights, and the futility of the prescriptions that traditionally govern the length of the musical theme, the number of its repetitions and the way it is developed. And that critique respects the foundations of both society and art: the tonal aesthetic remains the natural law of all music, property the natural law of all community. I have, naturally, no intention of explaining tonal music in terms of the regime of property ownership: I merely point out that there are, in every age, deep correspondences between the objects on which, in all fields, negativity exerts itself, and between the limits that negativity runs up against, at the same time, in all directions. 'There is a human nature, do not tamper with it!' Such is the shared signification of social and artistic prohibitions in the late eighteenth century.

Oratorical, pathos-laden and, at times, long-winded, Beethoven's art offers us, with a little delay, the musical image of the revolutionary Assemblies; it is Barnave, it is Mirabeau and, at times, alas, it is Lally-Tollendal. And I am not thinking of the *significations* he sometimes liked to give to his works, but of their *meaning*, which ultimately expressed his way of throwing himself into an eloquent, chaotic world. But, in the end, this torrential rhetoric and these floods of tears seem held in abeyance in a freedom of almost deathly calm. He did not overturn the rules of his art; he did not transgress its limits and yet one might say that he was beyond the triumphs of the Revolution, beyond even its failure. If so many people have chosen to seek consolation in music, it is, it seems to me, because it speaks to them of their troubles in the voice they will use to speak of them themselves once they have found consolation, and because it makes them see those troubles from the viewpoint of the day after tomorrow.

Is it impossible, then, today, for an artist, without any *literary* intention and any concern for *signifying*, to throw himself into our world with enough passion, to love it and hate it with such force, to live its contradictions with such sincerity, to plan to change it with such perseverance that that world—with its savage violence, barbarism, refined technologies, slaves, tyrants, deadly menaces and our fearful, imposing freedom— will transform itself, through him, into music? And if the musician has shared the fury and hopes of the oppressed, is it impossible for so much hope and rage to carry him beyond himself, so that he hymns this world today with a voice of tomorrow? And if this were the case, could we still speak of 'extra-aesthetic' preoccupations? Of 'neutral' subjects? Of signification? Could we distinguish the subject matter from its treatment?

It is to you that I put these questions, my dear Leibowitz, to you, not to Zhdanov. I know *his* reply, for,
just when I thought he was showing me the way, I
realized he was going astray. Hardly had he mentioned
overcoming objective reality when he added, 'In addi-
tion to this, the truthfulness and historical concrete-
ness of the artistic portrayal should be combined with
the ideological remoulding and education of the toil-
ing people in the spirit of socialism.' I had thought he
was inviting the artist to live the problems of the age
in their totality and to do so intensely and freely, so
that the work would reflect them to us in its own way.
But I see it is merely a question of ordering didactic
works from functionaries—works they will execute as
directed by the Party.

Since, instead of being allowed to find it, the artist
has his conception of the future imposed upon him,
it matters little that, where politics is concerned, this
future remains to be made; for the musician, it is
made already. The entire system sinks into the past.
Soviet artists, to borrow an expression they are fond
of themselves, are *backward-looking*; they hymn the
future of the USSR the way our Romantics hymned
the past of the monarchy. Under the Restoration,
it was a question of counterbalancing the immense
glory of our revolutionaries with an equal glory they
claimed to find in the early days of the *Ancien Régime*.
Today, the golden age has been shifted; it has been

projected into the future. But this roving golden age remains, nonetheless, what it was: a reactionary myth.

Reaction or terror? Art free but abstract, art concrete but encumbered? A mass audience that is uneducated, a specialist listenership, but a bourgeois one? It is for you, my dear Leibowitz, for you, who live out, in full awareness of what you do and without mediation or compromise, the contradiction of freedom and commitment, to tell us whether this conflict is eternal or just a moment in history and, if the latter is the case, whether the artist has in him today the means to resolve it or whether we have to wait for a profound change of social life and human relations to bring a solution.

Preface to René Leibowitz, *L'Artiste et sa conscience*
(Paris: Éditions de l'Arche, 1950)

✳

A NOTE ON SOURCES

'Materialism and Revolution'

Originally published as 'Matérialisme et révolution: I. Le mythe révolutionnaire' and 'Matérialisme et revolution: II. La philosophie de la revolution' in *Situations III*, NEW EDN (Paris: Gallimard, 2003), pp. 103–68.

First published in English translation in *The Aftermath of War* (London: Seagull Books, 2008), pp. 147–256.

'The Artist and His Conscience'

Originally published as 'L'Artiste et sa conscience' in *Situations IV* (Paris: Gallimard, 1964), pp. 17–37.

First published in English translation in *Portraits* (London: Seagull Books, 2009), pp. 15–44.